©Richard D. Irwin, Inc., 1993
The copyright on the compilation of this book is held by Richard D. Irwin.
The copyright on the individual articles is held by:
  The Times Mirror Company
  Times Mirror Square
  Los Angeles, CA 10017
and are used with permission. Contact them for permission to reprint.

All rights reserved. No part of this publication may be reproduced, stored in a retrieval system, or transmitted, in any form or by any means, electronic, mechanical, photocopying, recording, or otherwise, without the prior written permission of the publisher.

Printed in the United States of America.

ISBN 0-256-13325-5

2 3 4 5 6 7 8 9 0 ML 9 8 7 6 5 4 3

Applications of Fundamental Accounting Principles
Clippings from the *Los Angeles Times*
Kermit D. Larson
Paul B. W. Miller

Preface

This is the first edition of *Applications of Fundamental Accounting Principles*. These clippings from the *Los Angeles Times* are designed to accompany the 13th edition of FUNDAMENTAL ACCOUNTING PRINCIPLES. All of these articles were chosen to illustrate concepts that are covered in depth in the 13th edition. The articles were also chosen for their interest level and currency.

Each new copy of FUNDAMENTAL ACCOUNTING PRINCIPLES purchased from Irwin can come with a copy of this readings book. There will be no charge for *Applications of Fundamental Accounting Principles* in these instances. This supplement can also be purchased from Irwin separately for use with other texts or in other courses.

Our objective with these readings is to provide you, the instructor, with another way to demonstrate the usefulness of accounting information. The issues raised by these articles provide interesting new perspectives to many of the chapters in the 13th edition. Each of the articles is supported by at least one discussion question at the most appropriate point in the F.A.S.T. edition of FUNDAMENTAL ACCOUNTING PRINCIPLES. In addition to classroom discussions, the readings can also serve as a basis for additional assignments or independent study.

All of the articles are reproduced as near to their original appearance as is possible. This gives the reader a sense of their actual realism and may stimulate further learning and exploration beyond the timeframe of the introductory accounting course. This realism could not have been accomplished without the support of the people at the Los Angeles Times. Deserving of special thanks are Laura Morgan and Terri Niccum of the Media Relations Division.

We hope you enjoy this new teaching and learning tool.

Kermit D. Larson
Paul B. W. Miller

Table of Contents

Reading 1	"Accounting Firm Carves Out a Niche in Reviewing Records," *Los Angeles Times*, October 16, 1991.	1
Reading 2	"California Sues Outside Auditor in Lincoln Case," *Los Angeles Times*, June 28, 1990.	2
Reading 3	"Accounting Board Often Draws Wrath of Business," *Los Angeles Times*, December 21, 1990.	3
Reading 4	"A Road Map to Financial Planning," *Los Angeles Times*, September 19, 1990.	4
Reading 5	"Accounting Change Causes Quarterly Loss for Players," *Los Angeles Times*, November 12, 1991.	3
Reading 6	"Panel Backs Deukmejian on Budget Accounting Rules," *Los Angeles Times*, May 9, 1989.	5
Reading 7	"SEC Probe Adds to Landmark Land Co.'s Woes," *Los Angeles Times*, April 13, 1990.	6
Reading 8	"2 Firms Working on System to Speed Credit-Card Sales," *Los Angeles Times*, June 12, 1990.	7
Reading 9	"Checking Up on the Auditors: Accounting Firms Face Pressure to Do Their Job Better," *Los Angeles Times*, May 27, 1991.	8
Reading 10	"Accounting Firm Urges Torrance to Strengthen Investment Controls," *Los Angeles Times*, January 30, 1992.	10
Reading 11	"Audit Blasts DWP Accounting, Spending," *Los Angeles Times*, October 25, 1991.	11
Reading 12	"Money Store's Accounting: Holy Cow!," *Los Angeles Times*, October 7, 1991.	12
Reading 13	"Credit Where Credit's Due: Collecting Bad Debts Can Be a Lengthy Process. Prevention is the Better Strategy," *Los Angeles Times*, August 25, 1989.	13
Reading 14	"Community Psychiatric Centers Earnings to Drop," *Los Angeles Times*, November 5, 1991.	15
Reading 15	"End to 'LIFO' in Accounting Urged," *Los Angeles Times*, July 10, 1990.	16
Reading 16	"Accounting Demon Begone!" *Los Angeles Times*, May 6, 1991.	17
Reading 17	"Tax Ruling Could Put Squeeze on Developers' Cash Flow," *Los Angeles Times*, September 9, 1990.	19
Reading 18	"Board Proposes New Accounting Rules," *Los Angeles Times*, December 21, 1990.	21
Reading 19	"S&L Accounting Firm Partners Face Liability," *Los Angeles Times*, November 2, 1990.	22
Reading 20	"Making Taxes Work For You: CPA Helps Decode IRS Rules for Small-Business Owners," *Los Angeles Times*, March 12, 1990.	23
Reading 21	"Late Payments Cause Cash Flow Problem for Helionetics," *Los Angeles Times*, January 22, 1991.	26
Reading 22	"Optomistic Fluor Raises Quarterly Dividend by 25%," *Los Angeles Times*, December 12, 1990.	27
Reading 23	"AT&T's Puzzling Accounting," *Los Angeles Times*, September 16, 1991.	28
Reading 24	"Western Digital Sale of Network Unit Gets Final OK," *Los Angeles Times*, September 18, 1991.	29
Reading 25	"General Electric Co. Plans to Take $1.8-Billion Charge," *Los Angeles Times*, September 17, 1991.	30
Reading 26	"Sir Speedy Pays $4 Million for Accounting Franchiser," *Los Angeles Times*, September 18, 1990.	31
Reading 27	"Accounting Changes Aid Hammond," *Los Angeles Times*, May 16, 1990.	32
Reading 28	"Air Force Lied About B-1 Costs, GAO Study Says," *Los Angeles Times*, February 22, 1990.	33
Reading 29	"Effects Look Better on Screen Than Balance Sheet," *Los Angeles Times*, May 15, 1990.	34
Reading 30	"S&P Hits Planned Rule Change on Medical Benefits Accounting," Los Angeles Times, September 6, 1989.	36

BRIEFCASE

FINANCIAL SERVICES

Accounting Firm Carves Out a Niche in Reviewing Records

Like pathologists carving up a cadaver, a small Santa Ana accounting firm hopes to cash in on a little-known but growing and lucrative area of accounting that carves up past deals to find out what really happened.

Sparks & Nelson, a firm with six certified public accountants, is focusing its small office on what is called forensic accounting. But the firm is not alone.

"Forensic accounting is like the 'Quincy' of the bean-counting profession," said David S. Hanson, partner in charge of litigation support services in the Newport Beach office of Coopers & Lybrand. "It's somewhat sexy and unique, and every case is different. And, because of the nature of what you do, there's more money in it."

Forensic accounting, usually aimed at helping lawyers prove their cases, refers to situations where there is sketchy data, incomplete financial documents or even deliberately falsified information.

The forensic accountant reconstructs transactions, verifies and discovers information and generally

The Big 6 accounting firms, as well as most large accounting firms, have forensic accountants as part of their litigation support services departments. Such services have been a growing part of the accounting industry for more than a decade.

Sparks & Nelson, though, is devoting most of its manpower to forensic accounting. Partner John Nelson, for instance, has looked into a company's records to find out if one of its partners was cheating another. He found that his client wasn't cheated, but he discovered a loan on which his client was due interest.

For a businessman permanently injured in a fall, the accounting firm reviewed the man's tax returns and other information to estimate what his future income would have been and then provided expert testimony on the man's expected loss for being unable to work.

That sort of help is the bread-and-butter of forensic accounting and litigation support, Hanson said.

tries to provide the missing pieces, Hanson said.

"Any good CPA with a good background and good concept of business practices could be a good forensic accountant," he said. "But in terms of textbooks or programs, it doesn't exist. It's not something that's taught in college. It's basically a body of knowledge one gains through work."

—Compiled by James S. Granelli
Times staff writer

California Sues Outside Auditor in Lincoln Case

■ **Accounting:** The firm that merged to become Ernst & Young is accused by the state attorney general of helping defraud investors out of $250 million.

By NANCY RIVERA BROOKS
TIMES STAFF WRITER

State Atty. Gen. John K. Van de Kamp filed suit Wednesday against Arthur Young & Co., charging that the accounting firm helped defraud thousands of investors who bought more than $250 million worth of American Continental Corp. bonds.

The bonds are now worthless, and American Continental has filed for bankruptcy protection. Arthur Young was the company's independent auditor and has since merged with Ernst & Whinney to become Ernst & Young.

Also named in the suit were Charles H. Keating Jr., chairman of American Continental; other officers and directors of the company, which is the parent of Irvine-based Lincoln Savings & Loan, and Jack Atchison, an Arthur Young accountant who handled the American Continental account and then joined the Phoenix-based company at a much higher salary.

But Van de Kamp made clear that the main target of the suit is the accounting firm, partly because the other defendants have been the subject of more suits.

Accounting firms functioning as independent auditors have been much criticized for failing to more closely scrutinize thrifts that have since run into financial trouble, and some accounting firms have been banned by the federal Resolution Trust Corp. from working on thrift reorganization cases. But accounting firms have complained that they are being made scapegoats for the S&L crisis.

"If investors had known the truth, no one would have invested a dime in those bonds," Van de Kamp said at a news conference in Los Angeles. "But with Arthur Young standing behind them, their bonds sold easily."

The suit contends that the accountants failed to follow standard procedures, thereby making American Continental look healthier than it was. In 1987, financial statements prepared by Arthur Young show American with operating earnings of $27 million when the company actually lost $30 million to $50 million, Van de Kamp said.

An Ernst & Young lawyer vehemently denied the charges.

"We categorically reject the assertion that our work did not comply will all professional standards," said Eugene Erbstoesser, associate general counsel for Ernst & Young. "We stand behind our audit work. While it may be a long and arduous process, we believe we will be vindicated."

The suit, filed in Orange County Superior Court, seeks full restitution of the more than $250 million lost by more than 20,000 people, many of them elderly investors who bought the bonds through Lincoln Savings. The suit also seeks civil penalties, which Van de Kamp estimated could range between $50 million and $100 million, and attorney fees and suit costs. Van de Kamp is also asking for an injunction blocking the allegedly unfair business practices of the defendants.

"Charles Keating and his associates at American Continental Corp. were running a huge financial con game and sucking the assets out of Lincoln Savings to sustain their operations," Van de Kamp said. American Continental "engaged in a transparent series of sham real estate transactions and other unfair business practices designed to hide its true financial picture," and the company's auditor should have known about them, he said.

Lawyers for American Continental, which was not named in the suit, accused Van de Kamp of "grandstanding."

Noting that the state Department of Corporations filed a suit in March, American Continental lawyer James J. Feder said, "It looks to us like a waste of time, effort and taxpayers' money in a duplication of efforts.

"There's a different name on the top [of the suit] so some other politician can say they're protecting the public," Feder said.

Atchison's lawyer could not be reached. Bondholder lawyers had a mixed reaction.

"I welcome the attorney general, but where has he been for the last year?" asked Joseph W. Cotchett Jr., a Burlingame lawyer who is co-lead counsel for bondholders.

William S. Lerach, a San Diego lawyer who is the other co-lead, called the suit "duplicative and unnecessary."

"If more tax dollars are to be spent litigating against Mr. Keating, they should have been spent

(Continued on page 36)

Accounting Board Often Draws Wrath of Business

As the main rule-making body of the accounting profession, the Financial Accounting Standards Board has sometimes been a magnet for controversy.

The FASB is a sort of think tank made up of about 40 staff accountants and others "who possess knowledge of accounting, finance and business." Its rule-making body is a seven-member board that spends five days a week contemplating current accounting rules and how they can be changed to better reflect companies' true financial health.

Although the FASB is a private organization, the Securities and Exchange Commission enforces its dictates.

However, the board comes in conflict with business and industry at times, because it is constantly reviewing the way things are done. When the FASB decides that regulatory accounting rules or industry practice tend to mislead investors, it changes the rules.

Companies can protest proposed rules. But the FASB is supposed to base its final decision on accurate reporting—not industry wants. The only time it will succumb to less-than-ideal reporting standards is when the expected costs of implementing the rules exceeds the benefits, according to the organization's mission.

—KATHY M. KRISTOF

Accounting Change Causes Quarterly Loss for Players

Players International Inc. in Calabasas reported a $3.72-million loss for its fiscal second quarter because of an after-tax charge of $3.80 million stemming from an accounting change.

The loss came despite a 29% increase in Players' revenue for the quarter ended Sept. 30, to $5.80 million from $4.51 million a year earlier, when Players had a profit of $127,600.

Players operates the Players Club, which provides members with discounts at casinos and other recreation centers. It is also planning to operate a riverboat casino in the Midwest.

The charge reflects its decision to amortize its costs of obtaining new members of the Players Club over the initial membership period for new members—one year. Its previous practice was to amortize the costs over three years, Players said.

"This change in amortization for Players Club is more consistent with the accounting treatment of our other businesses," Players Vice Chairman David Fishman said in a statement.

For the first half of its fiscal year, Players lost $3.65 million compared with a year-earlier profit of $431,000, and its six-month revenue jumped 42%, to $12.5 million from $8.81 million.

A Road Map to Financial Planning

■ **Budgeting:** Some families, experts say, neither know where they stand financially nor where the bulk of their income goes. A cash-flow statement can remedy that.

By ALBERT B. CRENSHAW
THE WASHINGTON POST

WASHINGTON—A financial plan is a road map to get you from where you are to where you want to be economically—to a new home, a comfortable retirement, that sort of thing.

But to get from here to there, you have to know where here is. And to a surprising degree today, people do not know where they stand. In particular, they do not know where their money goes.

As a result, they can do no financial planning because neither they nor their planner, if they hire a professional, knows what they have to work with.

"It's really a common problem and really a significant problem," said William Brennan, a personal-finance expert with the accounting firm of Ernst & Young here.

The key to getting a handle on expenses, said Brennan and other financial planners, is a budget, or, more realistically, a cash-flow statement.

This requires a little effort, but it is well worthwhile. Planners differ on the exact time frame and whether to do it prospectively or retrospectively, but the basic idea is this: You pick a time period—three months or longer—and record all your expenditures. You can begin now and do it into the future, or you can sit down with your checkbook and other receipts and look back.

> 'I don't want to engage in too much pop psychology, [but] people who are working really hard tend to want to reward themselves' by spending money on things like vacations and eating out.
>
> DENNIS M. GURTZ
> *a financial planner*

What you are looking for is the leaks—all those little and perhaps not so little expenses that add up to the missing link in your income. Brennan said he commonly sees clients who think they know their income and outlays, but when they put them down on paper "a huge pot of money is unaccounted for."

"What's particularly interesting is the clients who, when they first sit down, say they don't have any money, no cash, no investments, but after expenses, they should have a huge amount left over," Brennan said.

"We say, 'Are you sure this is all the expenses? You should be saving $25,000 a year.'"

Of course, the answer is that the client is spending a lot of money without really being aware of it, at least not what it adds up to. That is where the cash-flow statement comes in. By tracking outlays carefully, day by day, it becomes clear where the extra is going.

And what do planners find is eating up the cash?

"The key word is *eat*," said Dennis M. Gurtz of Dennis M. Gurtz & Associates, a planning firm here. "Around here you may have two earners; [there] may be fairly heavy restaurant expenditures."

In addition, he said, "I don't want to engage in too much pop psychology, [but] people who are working really hard tend to want to reward themselves" by spending money on things like vacations and eating out that "bring personal release from the job."

Busy people also will spend extra for convenience, he noted. But there is a risk of getting caught in "sort of a circular formula—'I'm working so hard I have to have this housekeeper,'" then they have to work even harder to pay for that, Gurtz said.

Tracking all this down isn't especially hard. For the computer literate, there are a number of software programs that are designed to create cash-flow statements, balance sheets and other financial records. You also can do it on an ordinary spreadsheet program.

But really all you need is pencil and paper.

Lay out columns for the categories of expenses you incur and enter them each day or as often as you can. It's not crucial to get every penny, but if you put in your cash outlays each day and enter your checks from time to time, you will soon know where your income is going.

Once you know that, then you can begin your real financial planning.

And it will help you with other decisions. Once you see how much you are spending on, say, life insurance, you can decide if that's the right proportion of your income or whether you might be better off cutting your insurance somewhat and putting the savings into a savings plan or mutual fund.

"It gives [people] the ability to make rational decisions because they now have the facts in hand," Brennan said.

Panel Backs Deukmejian on Budget Accounting Rules

By DOUGLAS P. SHUIT, *Times Staff Writer*

SACRAMENTO—Hopes by Gov. George Deukmejian that the Commission on State Finance would put to rest the "accountants' debate" over the existence of a deficit in last year's budget ended Monday in a flurry of political sniping between Democratic and Republican lawmakers.

In between the political barbs, the commission voted 4 to 1 on a balanced budget resolution, saying in effect that the state budget has a "surplus" when revenues exceed expenditures in any given year.

The commission also recommended to the Legislature that for purposes of budget decisions, expenditures should not be counted until goods or services are actually delivered to the state.

Basically, the resolution supports Deukmejian's argument that the state ended the 1987-88 fiscal year in the black. Deukmejian's budget assessment was based on money raised and spent during the year, not on outstanding bills.

But the resolution did nothing to settle the large political fight that began months ago when state Controller Gray Davis and others charged that the Republican governor was hiding a deficit by resorting to accounting gimmicks.

The governor's critics noted that the state had spent much more money during the 1987-88 fiscal year than it had raised in tax revenues. The state got away with it because some of the goods it ordered were not actually delivered until the following budget year, the critics said.

The four members of the commission who voted in favor of the resolution backing up the governor's position were Republicans. The only "no" vote was cast by Controller Davis, a Democrat.

Seeing the handwriting on the wall before the vote, Davis fumed, "This is just a game. We are not doing anything serious or substantive."

Davis said the resolution "is clearly an attempt to save face by Gov. Deukmejian."

"We can get four votes that it will rain beer. That doesn't mean it will rain beer," Davis said.

Assemblyman William P. Baker (R-Danville) in turn scolded Davis. "I'd be very happy not to ever have accounting principles if you'd stop issuing press releases saying we're going broke," Baker said.

After the meeting, Sen. Ken Maddy (R-Fresno) was asked what he thought had been accomplished by the resolution and the hours of debate that had preceded it.

"Nothing . . . zero," Maddy said.

Another member of the commission, Assemblyman John Vasconcellos (D-San Jose), chairman of the Assembly Ways and Means Committee, who did not vote on the resolution, said the Republicans seemed to "have found a way of making it look like we have more money"—at least until 1990, when Deukmejian has announced that he will leave office. Then, Vasconcellos said, "the next governor will have to pick up the pieces."

The composition of the seven-member commission is prescribed by state law. It consists of the state treasurer, controller, finance director, two state senators and two assemblymen. GOP members gained a majority this year, when Republican Thomas W. Hayes was appointed to replace the late Jesse M. Unruh, a Democrat, as treasurer.

SEC Probe Adds to Landmark Land Co.'s Woes

■ Real estate: An investigation into its accounting practices is the golf course developer's latest regulatory problem.

By TOM FURLONG
TIMES STAFF WRITER

The problems are mounting at Landmark Land Co., the nationally recognized golf course developer whose operations have been hammered by growing losses in recent months.

The Carmel, Calif.-based firm recently disclosed in public documents that it is under investigation by the Securities and Exchange Commission for questionable accounting practices on a land deal last year near Palm Springs.

In connection with the probe, the firm said it may have to postpone taking more than $24 million in profits on the sale. A deferral would boost Landmark's losses in 1989 to $61.7 million and wipe out its shareholders equity, the firm said in its annual 10-K report on file with the SEC.

Landmark's SEC problems are the latest in a series of woes that include major losses in a savings and loan subsidiary from repossessed mobile homes, real estate foreclosures and junk bond write-offs, the firm has disclosed.

The firm also is a victim of last year's thrift bailout law, which in effect cut off a major source of funding, forcing it to sell or refinance its prime properties.

Landmark Land owns about two dozen golf courses around the country—including Mission Hills, PGA West and La Quinta in the Palm Springs area—as well as a savings and loan in New Orleans, known as Oak Tree Savings, that financed Landmark's extensive development activities.

Landmark also has developed major properties in Louisiana, Oklahoma, Florida, South Carolina and throughout California. It has major developments under way in California near Riverside, Sacramento and Redlands.

Landmark is known in sporting circles as one of the nation's premier developers of high-end golf courses. One of its best-known properties is the Oak Tree Golf Club near Oklahoma City, where the 1988 PGA golf championship was played.

The company's principal shareholder is Gerald G. Barton, a 58-year-old native Oklahoman who owns about 29% of Landmark's stock. Another major shareholder is Olympia & York Developments, the Toronto real estate company, which owns 25%.

The company's stock, traded on the American Stock Exchange, has been extremely volatile, trading as high as $22.625 and as low as $6 a share in the past year. Ignored by most financial analysts, the stock closed Thursday at $17.50 a share, up $2.125. Landmark suspended its dividend last December.

Barton has run Landmark, a one-time sugar company that had major real estate holdings, for about 20 years, making money by developing golf courses—surrounded by residential homes—for a wealthy elite who spend weekends in tony places such as Palm Springs and Carmel.

"His basic premise was there is an affluent set of people who will pay astronomical prices for premier golf courses and the houses around them," said Kenneth D. Campbell, president of Audit Investments, an investment advisory firm in Montvale, N.J.

The company, however, ran into deep trouble last year after Congress passed tough bailout legislation for the S&L industry that placed severe restrictions on thrift investment in real estate developments.

The law shut off Landmark's funding from Oak Tree Savings and is forcing the thrift to divest itself of more than $1 billion in real estate assets, according to Landmark Vice President Doug Barton, Gerald Barton's son. The senior Barton was not available for comment.

The company hopes to sell most of these properties, or restructure their loans, by the end of 1990, the younger Barton said in a phone interview. Landmark already has an agreement to sell its luxurious Carmel Valley Ranch Resort to American International Golf Resorts for $60 million.

Landmark's problems with the SEC arose after it recognized a $24.3-million profit in 1989 on a vacant piece of land near the PGA West golf course that it had sold to a real estate syndication company.

Regulators from the federal Office of Thrift Supervision, however, objected to the way the loan was structured, pointing out that the property's down payment came from Oak Tree Savings. Regulators don't want Landmark to recognize the full profit until additional payments on the Oak Tree loan are received.

Both Landmark and its outside auditor, Price Waterhouse, have objected to the OTS interpretation, and it's up to the SEC to decide who is correct, Doug Barton said. The accounting dispute has also sparked a shareholder lawsuit.

The OTS also wants Landmark to increase its reserves for loan losses by another $48 million on other development loans, including one on the La Quinta Hotel.

BRIEFCASE

SCIENCE/TECHNOLOGY

2 Firms Working on System to Speed Credit-Card Sales

Credit card purchases could soon take less time than cash transactions as a result of an agreement signed recently between two Irvine companies.

Trintech USA, a start-up subsidiary of Trintech International of Dublin, Ireland, and CUE Network Corp., a paging company, have agreed to establish a data transmission system they say will allow instantaneous verification for credit-card purchases.

With the credit-card verification procedure most retailers use, a clerk runs a customer's card through a point-of-sale machine. The machine dials a central computer, often at a bank, that contains a list of all bad credit cards. Next, a computer checks whether the customer's card is otherwise valid and whether the transaction is permitted, and it then notifies the point-of-sale machine with a verification or a rejection.

The whole process takes about 15 seconds, most of which is the time involved in setting up the phone call to the central computer. During the holiday shopping season, the transaction can take longer because many more retailers will be using the verification system.

Trintech USA's Xchecker point-of-sale system, now in the testing phase, will eliminate the need for the phone call and reduce the time needed for credit card verification to a few seconds, said Gene Swanzy, chairman and chief executive.

CUE will supply the radio communications link that will allow banks to store the computerized list of roughly 500,000 invalid cards in Trintech's point-of-sale machines. Using CUE's radio paging technology, the database can be sent to the machines and updated daily, said Leo Jedynak, CUE vice president of product development.

Swanzy said the system should lower retailers' costs by providing faster access to credit information and by reducing staffing and telephone expenses.

The point-of-sale terminals, which were developed in the United Kingdom by Trintech's parent company, will be manufactured for Trintech by a Finnish company, Swanzy said. Initial tests will verify MasterCard transactions.

With speedier verification, Jedynak hopes that the new verification system will encourage the use of credit cards for small sales such as meals at McDonald's and movie tickets.

"Since cash transactions often involve giving change, we can make using credit cards more convenient than cash," Jedynak said.

Checking Up on the Auditors
Accounting Firms Face Pressure to Do Their Job Better

The Big 6 accounting firms of Ernst & Young, Arthur Andersen & Co. and Deloitte & Touche are among the prime defendants in civil lawsuits arising out of the 1989 collapse of Lincoln Savings & Loan in Irvine.

Last week, another of the nation's Big 6 accounting firms, KPMG Peat Marwick, became the latest target of the much-vaunted crackdown by federal savings and loan regulators on such professionals as accountants and lawyers.

Peat Marwick is accused of a conflict of interest because a partner in charge of auditing a San Francisco thrift took out $1.7 million in loans from that thrift over the last five years. The accountants involved with Lincoln are accused of negligence in preparing financial statements for the S&L and its parent, American Continental Corp. in Phoenix.

WAYMOND RODGERS
Q&A

Across the nation, accounting firms are under a microscope as the government and investors who lost money seek compensation from deep-pocketed professional companies for alleged wrongdoing.

And the plaintiffs are winning big. Regulators are expected to collect more than $40 million in a pending settlement with Ernst & Young over its audits of Lincoln.

With the industry under pressure, the profession is looking for better ways of auditing firms—especially financial institutions—and ferreting out negligence and fraud, and of better informing the public about companies' financial affairs.

Waymond Rodgers, assistant professor of accounting at UCI's Graduate School of Management, has been studying how commercial lending officers make decisions on whether to fund loans and what techniques could be used to improve those decisions. He is also looking at accountants who audit financial institutions to find ways to improve their effectiveness.

In an interview with Times staff writer James S. Granelli, Rodgers talked about the problems the profession faces today and some of the solutions.

Q. Do independent auditors have a more difficult job with banks and savings and loans than with other industries?

A. They would probably have somewhat of a more difficult task in that banking is the most regulated industry in this country. That's mainly because the biggest area to audit by outside auditors is the loan portfolio, or, more specifically, the loan loss reserve. I was a commercial lending officer at one time, and I can tell you that quite a few loans that are made are based on qualitative features. Those qualitative features are often based on the managerial ability of the company that you're loaning the money to.

Q. In other words, you're looking to the character of the borrower, to a great extent, to determine if that person is reliable and will repay the loan?

A. Yes, exactly. What auditors, especially those who have not had experience as commercial lending officers, are looking at is certain factors that will perhaps suggest that the company borrowing money is a good bet or bad bet to repay the loan. Now, even though auditors may spot certain borrowers who are somewhat questionable in terms of the company being able to pay back its loan, they report their findings to a committee that consists of both the auditors and the clients—in this case, the top officials of the bank. At this point, certain negotiations take place. For instance, certain loans that the auditor may have classified as doubtful to be paid back, the bank officers have a chance then to question whether the auditors are properly classifying that loan.

Q. How independent are independent accountants if the result of their auditing stems from a negotiation with company executives?

A. They're very independent. If the auditors don't have enough information to change their mind about classifying a loan, then the client has the opportunity to provide some more information or insight about that particular borrower. This doesn't happen only in banking. It happens with other companies as well. That's pretty normal.

Q. But considering the large fees that accountants get for auditing, are independent auditors really independent or are there conflicts between their duties and their meal tickets?

A. I would say that the fees generally do not have any relationship with auditor independence. That is, even though some of these fees are very high, auditors still have a legal relationship with the client's board of directors that requires them to do the very best within their ability to audit that firm.

Q. To continue getting those fees, though, they have to continue a relationship with that company over the years. At what point is there concern that the auditor becomes too close to a company and begins to adopt the company's view of things rather than an independent view?

A. That does not necessarily happen. Auditors abide by a set of generally accepted auditing standards, and the way they approach an audit is predicated on these auditing standards. The program they use to audit companies is somewhat independent of the fees they charge or the length of time they've been auditing the firm. In fact, I would say that the longer they audit the firm, the better off they are in terms of understanding certain nuances of the firm. They can tailor that audit program to the specific firm.

Q. You'd probably get a lot of argument from the people who were bondholders in American Continental about whether the accounting firms were really independent.

A. Well, this doesn't necessarily apply to the Lincoln/American Continen-

(Continued on page 9)

(Continued from page 8)

tal case, but there are instances where accountants are pressured internally into not doing a thorough job. They have to complete audits within a certain time period, and that's tied to profitability. If an audit team stays close to the hours budgeted for a particular company, the accounting firm makes a bigger profit. If they take more time, the profit is smaller.

Q. What duties does an auditor owe to a company, to the shareholders, to the investing public and to the public in general?

A. The Securities Act of 1933 established that in terms of the auditors' liability for ordinary negligence, the onus is on the company and the accountants to show that the audit fairly represents the financial condition of the company. And the Securities Exchange Act of 1934 has provided a watchdog regulatory agency, the Securities and Exchange Commission, to enforce the 1933 act. However, today, auditors realize their potential liability for ordinary negligence has extended beyond their clients. Third parties, such as lenders or even potential investors, can in some cases successfully litigate against auditors. Court cases in California and about half the states in the past several years have emphasized that auditors' liability is not only to their client but to the third party as well.

Q. Does the accountant have a duty to look for fraud?

A. In fact, there have been two generally accepted auditing standards adopted in 1989 to deal with irregularities as well as to detect illegal acts by companies. The first deals with errors and irregularities of the companies. Errors pertain to material misstatements, unknown to the client, that may affect the judgment of someone reading that statement. Irregularity indicates that the client is doing something intentional, perhaps window-dressing figures, or even fraud. There is a statement, a guideline, a blueprint, so to speak, that auditors must follow in order to try to uncover those errors and irregularities.

❝ It is the auditor's responsibility to detect and report illegal acts by the client. ❞

The second standard states that it is the auditor's responsibility to detect and report illegal acts by the client.

Q. Reported to whom?

A. It depends. If the illegal act is performed by the treasurer or president or some top officer, then the auditor will report the act to the client firm's board of directors. If it's the board that has performed the illegal act, then the auditor is well advised to contact his own attorney.

Q. How often does an accountant really find illegal activity?

A. It's a very small amount. I would say that for those auditors who perform a very good audit, these fraudulent activities should pop out. It's darn near impossible for auditors to catch every illegal act by the client.

Q. What about catching any illegal act?

A. Yes, auditors have caught clients engaged in illegal acts. If they're doing a good audit, they should pick up an illegal act, if one has been committed. Auditors have discovered, for example, computerized banking fraud, check-kiting and lapping, which is where the client will take one customer account that has been paid on and apply the payment to another customer account to make it look as if the account is a good one.

Q. How is the average citizen able to read an audited financial statement and determine whether a financial institution is likely to fail?

A. There are 12,860 banks, quite a few of which are not audited. For those that are audited and are given a clean bill of health, the auditors did a very good job and those banks are performing quite well. There is a very small number of so-called problem banks. A recent study done by Veribanc Bank Rating Service indicated the problem banks on their list dropped to 301 from 314. So if you look at it from a broad picture—that is 12,860 banks of which 300 are problem banks—you're dealing with a very small percentage.

Q. Enough problems, however, to bankrupt the federal deposit insurance fund.

A. Yes, they're recapitalizing the Federal Deposit Insurance Corp., but that is due to other problems not related to audits made by CPA firms.

Q. But is there any effort by the industry to present financial statements that are understandable to the average person?

A. Yes, there is a great deal of work being done to try to get financial statements more user-friendly. In fact, there are certain research foundations that are funded exclusively by the Big 6 auditing firms, like the Peat Marwick Mitchell Foundation, which has given several million dollars to research and improve auditing techniques. The bottom line is to find a way to report information in such a way that makes it more user-friendly.

Q. What is the biggest issue facing auditors today?

A. I would say coming up with a better audit. We need to improve decision-making techniques, to improve auditors' understanding of certain clients and to report the client's operation and financial position as reflected by the numbers.

Q. Why is that issue more important now than it was 10 or 15 years ago?

A. I would say it was always important. But it's my opinion that auditors are being placed increasingly in the position of defending the way they audit, especially since they now may be liable to third parties led by class-action lawyers looking for deep pockets. Part of the

❝ Auditors are being placed increasingly in the position of defending the way they audit, especially since they now may be liable to third parties led by class-action lawyers looking for deep pockets. ❞

problem today is that we are in a more litigious environment. If there's any money to be found by a shareholder looking to recoup his lost investment, there are attorneys out there who will try to advocate that cause. Now that's not to say that happens all the time. Surely, there are some cases where the auditors did not do a thorough audit . . . and should be held liable.

Q. Are you saying that the state of litigation in the last few years has spurred the industry into reviewing both its ethical and procedural standards more closely and to tighten them up?

A. Well, I would put it in a different light. I would say that due to the court rulings that have come out in the last several years, there has been an emphasis on third-party rights, as opposed to fiduciary relationships between the CPAs and their clients. Auditors are responding to those issues. This could be said about auditing in most industries that have gone through changes.

Q. Is there anything else the profession is doing today to correct these problems?

A. Yes. There are several things they are doing. One is selecting their clients more carefully, looking for those who work in industries that the auditors have knowledge about. For example, many auditors are not seeking S&L or even bank clients unless they have a

Accounting Firm Urges Torrance to Strengthen Investment Controls

By DEBORAH SCHOCH
TIMES STAFF WRITER

An accounting firm, citing the possible loss of $6 million in city money, is urging the city of Torrance to "take immediate and decisive steps" to strengthen controls over how its money is invested.

The report, submitted by the Connecticut firm of Deloitte & Touche, recommends that the city hire an experienced investment officer, improve internal controls and create more clear-cut rules for investing city funds.

The city commissioned the report after learning that $6 million of city money is missing in a scandal involving Steven Wymer, an Irvine-based adviser who handled investment accounts for Torrance and other California cities.

Wymer has pleaded not guilty to 30 counts of securities fraud and other charges. Torrance officials say it is not known if any, or part, of the $6 million in city money invested by Wymer will ever be recovered.

City officials have since been scrutinizing the way city money is invested and are looking for ways to provide more oversight over the investments.

The Deloitte & Touche report was issued Tuesday, four days after City Hall officials issued their own plan for reforming the investment process. Both plans would dilute the responsibilities of the city treasurer by involving more people in investment-related decisions.

Mayor Katy Geissert said Wednesday that the Deloitte & Touche report "dovetails quite nicely" with the city's own plan.

City Treasurer Thomas C. Rupert, who is currently responsible for investing city funds, said he does not expect the reforms to infringe on his authority. Rupert said he supports the auditors' recommendation for hiring a city investment officer, who he said would work in his office.

Meeting Tuesday night, the City Council voted 7 to 0 to move ahead with plans to restructure investment procedures. But it postponed acting on specific plans until it can discuss the recommendations at a special meeting next Tuesday.

Deloitte & Touche, an accounting and consulting firm based in Wilton, Conn., issued its 23-page report after reviewing investment polices and practices.

"Overall, we found the city needs to take immediate and decisive steps to implement new and strengthen existing controls over the investment function," the firm stated.

Although the firm does not directly attack the city's current process, it observed that "delegating complete investment responsibility to one office violates a fundamental principle of good control, i.e., separation of duties."

The report goes on to urge the city to assign staff members outside the city treasurer's office "a day-to-day role in providing internal controls," such as checking the accuracy of treasury reports.

It suggested that the new investment officer have "an educational background and experience in fixed-income and money-market investments." And it concurred in a city plan to form an independent Treasury Advisory Committee to step up investment controls.

Audit Blasts DWP Accounting, Spending

By FREDERICK M. MUIR
TIMES STAFF WRITER

City Controller Rick Tuttle on Thursday blasted the Department of Water and Power for sloppy accounting and deliberately ignoring his rulings on expenses.

In a report released Thursday, Tuttle listed of 11 findings in which his auditors detailed misuse of travel and expense accounts.

Deputy Controller Tim Lynch described the team's findings as "unusual and not routine."

"There are serious problems of internal controls," Lynch said.

In his report, Tuttle concluded, "the internal control policies and procedures . . . have weaknesses that could affect the security of DWP assets."

The audit grows out of Tuttle's longstanding scrutiny of DWP spending practices. In 1989 he refused reimbursement of $879 in expenses for six top DWP officials and their spouses for dinner at the Sheraton Grand Hotel. A year later he denied a $2,800 bill for a charter jet trip for then-DWP General Manager Norm Nichols.

In the current audit, the controller's office, which acts as a watchdog of the city's finances, reviewed three trust accounts maintained by the DWP for petty cash and travel expenses.

Tuttle found that cash balances in the various accounts were poorly managed. For example, the controller said that the failure to invest excess cash in one account cost the department $16,900 in lost interest last year.

Overall, Tuttle wrote, "the reliability and integrity of reported information is not adequate because of a lack of compliance with existing policies, procedures and regulations."

A DWP spokesman said that most of the violations were of a technical nature and involved no criminal wrongdoing. DWP spokesman Ed Freudenberg said that virtually all of the recommendations made by the controller during the course of the audit have already been implemented over the past few months.

But one area of continuing disagreement involves reimbursement of expenses that Tuttle found to be excessive.

In one case, Tuttle had denied reimbursement of expenses at a Denver restaurant for a party of DWP employees. But on the same day that Tuttle refused to authorize reimbursement for the expenses, the DWP issued a check to the employee for the full amount.

"The actions of the DWP ignored the authority of the controller to approve or deny the expenditure of public funds," said Tuttle in the report.

Lynch said the DWP action was not a mistake, but "was conscious and deliberate."

The tab for the Denver outing was not immediately available. DWP officials have defended the restaurant party as a legitimate expenditure. The matter is to go before the City Council for a determination sometime in the next few weeks.

In another case, an employee was given a $2,274 advance for travel expenses, and was then paid an equal amount again when he filed his accounting. Tuttle's auditors uncovered the double payment and the funds have now been returned by the employee.

The audit also found lax monitoring of outstanding advances. More than 63% of the cases checked were more than 120 days old, even though DWP policy requires for advances to be accounted for within 10 days. In two cases, Tuttle found that former employees had left the agency with outstanding advances totaling $281.

DEALS / ALLAN SLOAN
Money Store's Accounting: Holy Cow!

Holy Cow! If that phrase makes you think of a nasal drone instead of a sacred bovine, it means you're within the sound of the voice of Phil Rizzuto, the former New York Yankee shortstop and TV-radio announcer whose main public function these days is pitching for the Money Store Inc., one of the country's biggest second-mortgage companies.

Most of the United States, in fact, is within the sound of Rizzuto's voice. That's because Money Store, which makes student loans and Small Business Administration loans as well as second mortgages, operates in 32 states and the District of Columbia and spends a hefty $11 million a year—around 10% of revenue—on ads.

Last month, the company made the financial big leagues by selling $35 million worth of stock to the public. The shares, traded on the American Stock Exchange, have taken off like a Mickey Mantle home run. The company sold it for $16 on Sept. 20, it has never traded below $17.625 and it closed Friday at $20. That values the whole company at more than $150 million, and the stock owned by the biggest shareholders, the Turtletaub family of New Jersey, at more than $110 million. Holy cow! Not bad for a business the family started in 1967 when the second mortgage market, now respectable, had all the cachet of selling children into slavery.

What do you get when you fork over your dough to become the Turtletaubs' junior partner? A lot less than meets the eye, in my humble opinion.

Why do I say this? Because Money Store's cash flow statements show that although the company reports consistent profits, it's not clear how much money, if any, it's really making.

How can this be? In a word: accounting.

Using a perfectly legal method of keeping books, Money Store counts as current profits money that it expects to make in the future. If you subtract that item from reported profits, they pretty much disappear.

Let me explain. Money Store is in the business of making loans and selling them. Money Store makes you a second mortgage loan at, say, 12%, and sells it to a bank that is happy to collect 9.5% because Money Store does all the work and guarantees to buy the loan back if it goes sour.

The day Money Store sells the loan, it counts as profit the 2.5-point spread between what you pay and what it pays the bank, multiplied by the number of years it expects the loan to be outstanding, with a discount for the fact that these profits flow in over a period of years rather than all at once.

Economists call this the "present value" of the 2.5-point spread. Money Store calls it an "increase in excess servicing asset." That sounds much more impressive than "future profits we think we'll make."

Subtract the after-tax impact of this item, and 1988's $10.1-million profit becomes a $100,000 loss. The 1989 profit of $15.1 million becomes a $1.3-million loss. The 1990 profit of $8.1 million becomes a $1.6-million loss. The first half of 1991 shows a $2.1-million profit rather than the reported $5.3-million profit. It's counting your chickens before they hatch. Even though you will probably have chickens someday, all you have now is eggs.

Why is 1991 looking so much rosier? The company changed its loan sales methods to report more profits now and fewer later. For an example of how arbitrary this bookkeeping is, consider this. The company changed accounting in 1990 to conform with suggestions made by a national accounting task force. Using last year's accounting in 1988 and 1989 would have reduced reported profits by a third.

Now add in the fact mentioned above—that Money Store sells many of its loans with a guarantee to buy them back if they go sour. What's happening because of the recession and falling real estate values? Just what you would expect.

The company bought back $7.1 million in loans in 1988, $14.7 million in 1989, $21.8 million in 1990 and $14.1 million in the first half of 1991. Annualized, the 1991 rate is $28.2 million a year, but it wouldn't surprise me if the number exceeds $30 million by year-end. In other words, the company is buying back four times as many loans as it did in 1988, but its second mortgages have only doubled.

To be sure, not all these loans stay bad, and the ones that stay bad aren't necessarily total losses. Money Store charged against its profits $3.5 million for loan losses in 1988, $9.2 million last year and $6.1 million the first half of this year. But it takes cash to buy these loans back. Which may be why the company borrowed $55 million at a stiff 12% interest rate at the end of 1989. Selling stock strengthens the balance sheet enough to allow Money Store to borrow more money.

When I called Money Store headquarters in Union, N.J., to ask about all this, the company said its lawyers have advised it not to talk to me until December when the 90-day "quiet period" after its stock sale ends. Rizzuto didn't call me back, but hey, he's the pitcher, not the owner.

But I managed to find people who gave me Money Store's point of view. Which is this. Despite the non-cash nature of the company's

(Continued on page 36)

ALLAN SLOAN *is a financial columnist for Newsday in New York.*

SMALL BUSINESS / Jane Applegate

Credit Where Credit's Due

*Collecting bad debts can be a lengthy process.
Prevention is the better strategy.*

Debt collection. The words themselves have an ominous sound.

Yet, most small businesses are plagued with uncollected bills, which can hurt an otherwise healthy business. Attorneys and others who specialize in debt collection say even the boldest entrepreneur may have trouble demanding money owed him.

But collecting money from customers or clients does not have to be an onerous task if you develop a strategy, according to Reid L. Steinfeld, an attorney who specializes in collections at the Encino law firm of Weissman & Weissman.

After 10 years of collecting money owed a variety of businesses, Steinfeld has become a strong proponent of preventive medicine when it comes to debt collection.

The first step is to insist that the new customer fill out a detailed credit application unless he or she plans to pay cash on delivery. By demanding certain information up front, serious problems can be avoided later, Steinfeld says.

"At the beginning of a relationship, everyone loves each other," Steinfeld said. So this is when the small-business owner should collect all the financial and personal information needed to decide whether to extend credit.

Businesses can draft their own credit application or buy a standard form at a stationery store and adapt it to fit the company's needs.

The purpose of the form is to find out:

■ With whom has the company had business dealings before? Insist on a list of contacts, addresses and phone numbers, and be sure to verify references.

■ Where does the company have its bank accounts? What are the branch addresses and account numbers?

■ Does the customer or the company own any property? Where is the property, and is it mortgaged?

■ Can the debt be secured with a tangible asset such as the equipment you are selling the company or some other item of value?

■ Is the business owner willing to provide a personal guarantee for the money owed, even if the company is incorporated?

Then, before extending credit, *verify* everything on the application. Start by calling the companies listed and ask how the company seeking credit pays its bills. Check the owner's or company's credit rating through TRW or Dun & Bradstreet. Have the Secretary of State's office run what is called a "UCC (Uniform

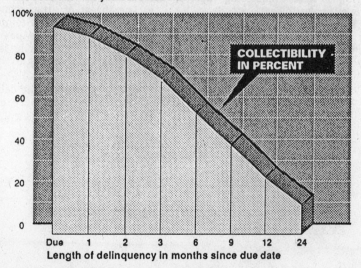

(Continued on page 14)

(Continued from page 13)
Commercial Code) search" to determine whether the company has any secured creditors. This affects how and when your company would be paid off if the other business fails.

Steinfeld also suggests adding a line or two on the credit application which states that any litigation stemming from the transaction must be filed in the city where *your* business is, rather than where the customer has his or her business. This will make life easier if you end up having to sue the company to recover your money.

To avoid disputes about whether goods were received, Steinfeld recommends following up each order with a brief confirmation letter detailing the products or services you provided.

What if you have checked the customer's references, called his bank and assured yourself that he is a good credit risk—and he still ends up owing you money?

"It becomes a race," said Steinfeld. "The longer you wait, the harder it is to collect." (See graph.)

If you have not been paid during the normal 30-, 60- or 90-day payment period, first write a letter requesting the money you are owed.

Then have your credit manager or other responsible person call the debtor. Based on experience, Steinfeld said debtors will either refuse to take your calls or launch into a long list of excuses about why they cannot pay you.

If they make excuses, Steinfeld suggests saying you are not interested in hearing them. Tell the debtor you sold him something in good faith and that you expect to be paid promptly. Tell him you have a business to run and your own payroll to meet.

"You have to be firm and positive," said Steinfeld. If the debtor is unwilling to work out a payment schedule, you may be forced to go to court.

At that point, most business owners turn to their attorney for help. If the debt is under $25,000, a business owner can seek help in municipal court. If the debt exceeds $25,000, the claim can be filed in superior court.

"You must take a strong legal position because debtors are much more sophisticated and know how to play the game better than ever," said Steinfeld.

If it is time to play hardball, Steinfeld said your attorney can help you obtain what is called a "prejudgment writ of attachment." A judge will issue such an order if he is convinced that you have a valid claim against the debtor. This type of court order permits you to freeze a company's assets and prevent any disposition until there is a hearing on the dispute.

"The threat of attachment is very powerful," said Steinfeld. He said many debtors pay up immediately after receiving legal notice that you are going to court to attach their assets.

"In our experience, the debtor either files for bankruptcy, calls to make a deal or hasn't got the money and doesn't care anymore," said Steinfeld.

He also reminds business owners that any three creditors can force a business into involuntary bankruptcy, but that can be an expensive proposition because of the legal fees involved.

"It's always best to try to make a deal because you can lose in court," advises Steinfeld.

Just how much money do businesses owe each other?

The Commercial Collection Agency section of the Commercial Law League of America keeps track of debts by polling 64 commercial collection agencies quarterly.

In the first quarter of this year, commercial receivables reached a record $720.6 million, represented by 450,000 claims, according to Bethesda, Md., attorney Gordon Calvert. The total dollar volume dipped to $715.9 million, represented by 396,620 claims, during the second quarter of this year. Calvert said the figures reflect the financial health of U.S. businesses and their ability to pay off their debts.

Community Psychiatric Centers Earnings to Drop

■ **Finance:** The Laguna Hills chain predicts a decline of about $14 million due to bad debts and bill-collection delays.

By DEAN TAKAHASHI
TIMES STAFF WRITER

LAGUNA HILLS—Community Psychiatric Centers said Monday that its fourth-quarter earnings will be reduced by about $14 million because of continuing losses from bad debts and delays in bill collection.

The Laguna Hills-based psychiatric hospital chain also said that its patient numbers and new admissions have dropped in the fourth quarter compared to a year ago. The company attributed the decline to the weak economy and tougher admissions-review policies by third-party providers such as health maintenance organizations.

Patient admissions since Sept. 1 have dropped 6% to 8% compared to a year earlier, the company said.

It also said admissions have been hurt by unfavorable media coverage about alleged fraudulent business practices involving Psychiatric Institutes of America, a private psychiatric hospital chain owned by National Medical Enterprises in Santa Monica.

The company said its business with health maintenance organizations has declined as HMOs negotiate lower rates and place tougher limits on the length of time a patient can be treated in psychiatric hospitals and still receive insurance reimbursement. HMOs account for about 35% of CPC's annual sales.

The company said the $14-million reserve should account for anticipated losses in accounts receivable as of Sept. 30. CPC's accounts receivable totaled $108 million as of Aug. 31, company spokeswoman Suzanne Hovdey said.

The company has already taken a $23-million reserve against its third-quarter earnings for billing problems.

CPC said its billing problems have been particularly bad in California, a competitive market that accounts for one-quarter of the company's hospital beds. Because of those problems, the company said that Richard L. Conte, president, will now oversee its 15 California hospitals.

The company's stock closed at $12.50 Monday, down $1.25 a share on the New York Stock Exchange.

CPC Chairman James Conte said the company has tabled its acquisition plans because of negative trends in the industry. In September, CPC made an offer valued by analysts at $350 million to acquire two Texas health-care companies. But the company dropped those plans after reporting a 98% decline in third-quarter earnings.

"They realize they will be busy cleaning their own house," said Joel Ray, an analyst at Kidder, Peabody & Co. in New York. "The whole industry is going through a shakeout."

In October, Psychiatric Institutes of America, a CPC competitor, was hit with allegations that some of its hospitals and treatment centers systematically misdiagnosed, mistreated and abused patients to increase its profits from insurance claims. The company has said it is not guilty of any wrongdoing and that the charges are inaccurate or overblown.

But CPC, which has not been accused of any wrongdoing, said it has been hurt by the unfavorable industry publicity.

The company said it is also looking for a full-time chief financial officer. It will also establish an internal audit department and a national accounts-receivable department in an effort to more closely monitor accounts receivable.

CPC operates 50 hospitals in 18 states with a total of 5,100 beds.

For the nine months ended Aug. 31, it reported earnings of $48.3 million on revenue of $311.2 million.

End to 'LIFO' in Accounting Urged

■ **Finance:** Many U.S. firms prefer the 'last in, first out' method of valuing inventory. But an international committee calls it misleading.

By GRAEME BROWNING
THE BALTIMORE SUN

BALTIMORE—The road to a global economy can be rocky even in the best of times. But as far as the U.S. accounting profession is concerned, a little-known international committee just rolled a boulder into the middle of a crucial turn.

The London-based International Accounting Standard Committee, a group formed by 13 industrialized countries in 1975 to formulate accounting principles that could be used worldwide, voted recently to recommend that LIFO—short for "last in, first out"—be eliminated as a method for valuing inventory.

The idea makes sense outside of the United States. Many countries consider LIFO a bad accounting practice because it inflates the value of inventory on a company's balance sheet.

But Americans bridle at the recommendation. Many U.S. companies prefer LIFO over its counterpart, FIFO, or "first in, first out," because it results in a lower tax bill.

Also, federal tax laws require U.S. companies to use LIFO in certain circumstances. The laws have been on the Internal Revenue Service books since 1937, and eliminating LIFO in the United States would take an act of Congress, said Arthur Wyatt, a senior partner with the Chicago accounting firm of Arthur Andersen & Co. and one of two U.S. delegates to the IASC. Congress "might be persuaded to do it if it seemed to be in the national interest, but that would be a battle to be fought in Washington and nowhere else," he said.

LIFO and FIFO are among the more arcane categories in accounting terminology, but the methods they describe are relatively simple.

In order to compute its earnings for the year, a company must put a value on the goods that remain in its inventory at year's end. With LIFO, all goods remaining in inventory are valued at the price last paid for them. With FIFO, the goods are valued at the price originally paid for them.

The difference in the methods is most apparent in an inflationary economy.

Under LIFO, the value of the inventory, and thus the amount of earnings, is lower. With FIFO the two figures are higher. The higher its earnings, the more taxes a company has to pay—and vice versa. If a company uses LIFO in computing its taxes, the Internal Revenue Service requires it to use LIFO in financial statements it prepares for investors, auditors and such federal agencies as the Securities and Exchange Commission. A company that uses FIFO for taxes can use either method for financial statements.

Many U.S. companies routinely elect LIFO over FIFO. Of 600 companies surveyed by the American Institute of Certified Public Accountants, the leading trade association for the accounting profession in the United States, more than 400 use LIFO for both tax and financial reporting.

Also, as the U.S. economy has become increasingly inflationary, LIFO has become the method of choice.

FIFO, its counterpart, "gives you the most profit in the good times and the most loss in the bad times," said Edward P. Brunner, vice president and chief financial officer of Baltimore Life Insurance Co.

In the past 20 years, the United States has "had several dips in the economy, and people who used FIFO got whipsawed. Companies changed to LIFO because they didn't want to get hit again," said Brunner.

DEALS / ALLAN SLOAN

Accounting Demon Begone!

EXORCIST WANTED: I have a pressing need to cast out a huge accounting demon. Big $$$$. Sense of humor helpful but not required. Contact M. Fromstein. Fee paid.

The help-wanted ad above may strike you as a little weird. But it's not as weird as the situation in which Mitchell Fromstein actually finds himself.

Fromstein, who is definitely a real person even though the ad is fictional, is the chairman of Manpower, the big temporary-help company based in suburban Milwaukee. The accounting demon, a huge and nasty beast, allowed a British company to successfully raid Manpower in 1987 and has clobbered Manpower's earnings since 1989, when Fromstein mounted a boardroom coup and took control of the British raider from within.

Exorcising the demon is a messy and expensive procedure that won't be over until 1993. Just the paper shuffling is costing more than $10 million.

A major step in the process is under way—but Manpower calls it an exchange offer rather than an exorcism. Holders are trading shares of Manpower PLC, a British company, for shares of Manpower Inc., a U.S. company. The company's business will stay the same. The company's headquarters, which were already in Milwaukee for all practical purposes, will now be there officially.

Fromstein, a funny, feisty 63-year-old determined to finish fixing the company before he retires, says his lawyers have ordered him not to talk until the Manpower-for-Manpower exchange is finished, which is scheduled May 13. The SEC, which regulates these things, isn't talking about the deal, either.

So this column is based on my reading of public documents and on interviews conducted before Manpower filed its exchange offer last month.

The point of Fromstein's maneuvering is to return Manpower to what it was before a British company called Blue Arrow raided it in 1987, using the differences between U.S. and British accounting to make sure no U.S. companies intervened. This difference created the accounting demon.

Blue Arrow, financed by demented banks caught up in takeover craziness, bid $1.3 billion in cash for Manpower and took over the company despite Fromstein's bitter opposition. Fromstein's efforts included the thankless task of trying to interest members of Congress in accounting. That's like trying to get 4-year-olds to eat spinach rather than ice cream. But it's rough poetic justice, considering that Fromstein once told me that he stayed as far away as he could from accounting because his father had been an accountant.

(Continued on page 18)

Demon Begone—*continued from page 17*

No U.S. company with publicly traded stock could match Blue Arrow's bid for Manpower because U.S. accounting rules would have forced the acquirer to take a big hit in his earnings—around $30 million a year for 40 years.

That's because of something called "goodwill." Goodwill is the difference between what you pay for a company and the value of its tangible assets like buildings and equipment.

Because Manpower had almost no tangible assets—a few desks, some machines, but no factories or inventory—almost everything you paid for it would go on the books as goodwill. Not so for British companies, which can write off the goodwill without charging it against earnings.

When a series of scandals got Blue Arrow's board to toss out its chairman, Fromstein, who had mounted a boardroom coup, ended up running Blue Arrow. He renamed it Manpower, sold most of the old Blue Arrow businesses, moved Manpower nee Blue Arrow back to Milwaukee. About 75% of the shares are now in the hands of U.S. citizens.

Blue Arrow had used British rules to write off the $1.3 billion of goodwill that it got from taking over Manpower. But it's clear that the SEC made Fromstein keep a U.S. set of books, goodwill included.

Somehow, Fromstein got the SEC to let him write off most of the goodwill in 1989 and to charge off the rest over five years rather than the traditional 40. I know that because buried in Manpower's exchange-offer documents is the information that Manpower took a special $1.1-billion writeoff of its goodwill in fiscal 1989 and began writing off the remaining goodwill over five years.

As a result, Manpower's goodwill charges, which will run about $80 million a year through 1993, are so large that securities analysts add them back into reported profits—or, in Manpower's case, subtract them from reported losses in order to produce profits.

It isn't clear how Fromstein got the SEC to let him do this. As I said before, neither Fromstein nor the SEC is talking.

Robert Willens, the Lehman Bros. tax and accounting genius who helped me crunch Manpower's numbers, says he's never seen a case like this before.

"This is most unusual," says Willens. "Normally, you can't write off goodwill unless you can prove that the businesses you acquired have had their value permanently impaired." Which Manpower's business obviously hasn't. Says Willens: "You can be sure I'll try to use this precedent for our clients."

So what we have here is Fromstein finding a way to artificially reverse the artificial accounting charges that let British buccaneers take over one of Milwaukee's most important corporations. A most complicated way to get back where you started. What's more, Fromstein seems to have the accounting demon pretty much buried. For accountants, this will be the bier that makes Milwaukee famous.

WASHINGTON / CATHERINE COLLINS
Tax Ruling Could Put Squeeze on Developers' Cash Flow

If real estate developers do not have enough to worry about with soft markets and a nationwide credit crunch, they can now fret over higher tax bills.

But their plight has a sympathetic ear in Washington. Sens. David Pryor (D-Ark.) and Steve Symms (R-Idaho) plan to introduce the Real Estate Fairness Act of 1990 on Tuesday in an attempt to allow developers to continue to calculate their taxes on economic gain as they have for decades.

The legislation is intended to address the Internal Revenue Service's recent reinterpretation of a 60-year-old law in a way that could double the tax bills of developers if not reversed.

Since 1928, the law governing the sale of subdivided land has held that estimated costs of future improvements may be included when establishing the basis of the sold property as long as the improvements are required by contract. It is fairly typical for a developer to operate with a negative cash flow in the early stages of a project. Initial sales then pay for the land improvements to come.

The IRS has decided that developers can no longer use the projected cost of land improvements to offset profits of the sale of their properties unless the improvements have been completed. This is the new interpretation even if the developers are obligated by contract to build roads, construct parks or install sewer lines.

In other words, in the past, if a developer paid $500 for a lot and resold the land for $1,000, while contracting to make $250 worth of

CATHERINE COLLINS is a Washington writer.

FRED SMITH / For The Times

improvements, he was liable for taxes on the $250 profit. Under the new IRS plan, he must pay taxes on the gain of $500 if the improvements have not been made.

"This couldn't come at a worse time," said Ken Kies, tax counsel for the American Resort and Residential Development Assn. "For many developers already caught in the credit crunch, cash flow is already a problem."

Tom Franks, senior vice president of the developers' trade group, said: "The interesting thing is that there has not been any pattern of abuse here. We see no justification to change a law that has worked fine for 50 years now."

"The situation is a real cash flow problem," said Jeff Trinca, Pryor's legislative aide. "Now, a developer's line of credit will have to include money to make improvements. Before, you could sell off a third of the lots to pay for the improvements on all. If the law says you have to improve the property up front before you can get the tax benefits, it will just add to the industry's problems."

Both the industry and the two senators hope that the problem can be ironed out at an IRS hearing scheduled for late October. If it cannot be solved by reinterpreting the regulations, the fight to restore the old way of doing it will move to Congress.

The Battle Rages Over Purchasing Law

The 1988 law regulating how the government spends $200 billion a year for everything from tanks to toothbrushes had hair on its chest. But within three months of its enactment, its provisions were suspended in the face of strong opposition, led by the defense industry.

Since then, Congress has waited for the Administration to write the regulations to implement the Procurement Integrity Law. But instead of new regulations, the Bush Administration has written a whole new bill that does away with the earlier law and has sparked a new debate.

The 1988 law is scheduled to go back into effect Dec. 1 unless Congress and the Administration can craft a compromise on new legislation or new regulations to implement the law. But those involved in the talks say that the sides are still far from agreement.

Sen. William V. Roth Jr. (R-Del.) introduced the Administration's new bill 2775, saying little more than "the Administration's proposal is a good starting point."

The Senate has tried to buy extra time to work out a deal by approving an amendment offered by Sen. Carl Levin (D-Mich.) to extend the suspension for another six months. But word from the House is that some members are upset with the

(Continued on page 20)

Tax Ruling—continued from page 19

Administration's tardy proposal and prefer not to act on Levin's measure. That would have the effect of reinstating the law on Dec. 1.

Two of the most influential House committee chairmen, Reps. John Conyers (D-Mich.) of Government Operations and Jack Brooks (D-Tex.) of Judiciary, are said to prefer the tougher provisions of the 1988 law over the Administration proposal.

Meanwhile, under pressure from Brooks and Conyers, the Administration published draft regulations for the existing law late last week.

The suspended law would do three major things. First, it would prohibit contractors or government employees from accepting gifts or gratuities during the course of a contract or employment. They would even have to bring their own coffee and bagels to meetings with outsiders.

Second, it would prohibit the release or acceptance of any sensitive inside information. And third, it would deal with the revolving-door issue by prohibiting government employees from working on contracts that they had negotiated for two years after leaving the government. It would not, however, prohibit a former employee from working for a private company on another contract.

The suspended law also had strict penalties. If caught violating the provisions, a company could forfeit its government contact and face debarment from further government business. Both companies and individuals involved also could face substantial fines.

The Bush Administration has complained about the "cumbersome, duplicative and burdensome structure" of the measure.

The White House proposal covers only the protection of inside information and leaves the issues of gifts, gratuities and the revolving door to existing criminal, civil, and regulatory prohibitions.

"The suspended law has enormous ambiguity and stifled communication between contractors and the government," said Lorraine Lavet, director of procurement policy at the U.S. Chamber of Commerce. "The chamber supports the Administration's package because of its clarity and simplicity. Yet it still has strong language. It is to our advantage in industry to be able to train our employees about exactly what they can and cannot do."

And from the other side, a congressional source said: "This whole system is based upon an open competitive environment where no company is favored over another. When a government employee receives gifts, however small, from the very people with whom he is negotiating a contract, it undermines the integrity of the system. If a contractor hears that a government employee was wined and dined by his competitor who won the contract, he is going to believe the worst, not that his competitor had the best product at the best price.

"When people start to believe that, it corrupts the system. The system runs on good faith and if its participants feel it is corrupt, they will behave accordingly."

Board Proposes New Accounting Rules

By KATHY M. KRISTOF
TIMES STAFF WRITER

In a flurry of activity this week, accounting rule makers announced plans to set standards that may cost individuals and industry billions of dollars.

The Financial Accounting Standards Board, an organization that sets rules for financial reporting at publicly held companies, sent out two separate "statements" advising companies and accountants of upcoming changes this week.

One such change will force companies to set up reserves for their employees' post-retirement medical benefits instead of paying these benefits out of current earnings, which is the general industry practice.

Some industry experts believe that if corporations did nothing to restrict their costs (that is, cut back on employee benefits), this rule could cut corporate profits by upward of $200 billion over a period of years.

The other rule is designed to give shareholders more current information about company-held investment portfolios. But company insiders and analysts complain that it will force financial institutions to spend millions hiring legions of actuaries and accountants to do nothing but comply with the proposed rule.

Neither rule will go into effect immediately. The medical benefit rule, for example, starts in 1993. And the other could be delayed even longer.

But already companies and their consultants are scrambling—trying to change their operations in ways that will make these rules less costly.

"This will have a significant impact on companies, their financial results and their employees," said Marsha Venturi, consulting actuary with Buck Consultants in Secaucus, N.J., about the retirement benefit rule. "When companies take a good look at how expensive those benefits are, they are going to start re-evaluating what they provide."

Already Venturi says several of her clients have changed benefit programs to limit their future expenses. Some are requiring retirees to ante up more per month for their own insurance, others are capping company-paid benefits and others are making working employees contribute more to pay for benefits they may collect when they retire.

In short, companies may find their earnings hit by the rule, but

> 'This will cost millions. Serious millions. Insurance companies would have to have appraisers on staff to re-evaluate every [shopping] mall.'
>
> JOYCE CULBERT
> Firemark Insurance Research

employees will feel the pinch, too, Venturi added.

Meanwhile, financial services companies are still trying to fight a proposed rule that would force them to disclose the current market value of their loans and investment portfolios in the footnotes of their financial statements.

Although these footnotes are generally read only by accountants, financial analysts and reporters, some complain that calculating the figure will require legions of accountants and actuaries.

The rules would apply to all companies, but banks, savings and loans and insurance firms would be most affected because they often hold large portfolios of loans and investments.

These assets are generally recorded on their books at their original purchase prices. The accounting rule makers want companies to say what the assets would be worth if they had to sell them today.

"This will cost millions. Serious millions," said Joyce Culbert, vice president of research at Firemark Insurance Research in Parsippany, N.J. "Insurance companies would have to have appraisers on staff to re-evaluate every [shopping] mall. And you'd need another horde of actuaries to figure out the present value of your insurance policies. This would be exceptionally costly."

Nevertheless, many industry observers favor the new rules because they say they will give investors a better picture of a company's true financial health. Post-retirement benefits can be a huge liability. And if it is not disclosed, investors could be blindsided when a company is forced to start paying these benefits from current earnings.

Moreover, financial services regulators have been widely criticized for allowing "once-upon-a-time" accounting of investment portfolios.

Accounting standards that didn't require up-to-the-minute disclosure of what assets were worth were cited as a major problem in the savings and loan debacle. Some experts maintain that regulators simply didn't know how sick some thrifts had become because accounting rules didn't force them to disclose when their investments had soured.

S&L Accounting Firm Partners Face Liability

By JAMES S. GRANELLI
TIMES STAFF WRITER

A judge overseeing civil suits relating to the failure of Lincoln Savings & Loan ruled Thursday that partners in three major accounting firms are individually responsible for any damage awards investors may win.

U.S. District Court Judge Richard M. Bilby in Phoenix certified as class-action defendants the partners of Arthur Young & Co., Arthur Andersen & Co. and Touche, Ross & Co. Only partners with the firms when they represented American Continental Corp.—roughly from 1984 to April, 1989—are included.

Arthur Young and Touche Ross have since merged with separate firms and are now Ernst & Young and Deloitte & Touche.

American Continental, which owned Irvine-based Lincoln, went bankrupt in April, 1989, and regulators seized the S&L. Thousands of investors lost more than $250 million from American Continental's collapse, and the thrift's failure is expected to cost taxpayers more than $2 billion.

Bilby's decision puts at risk the assets of nearly 4,000 individual partners at the three firms, giving plaintiffs—many of whom lost their life savings in American Continental bonds—another avenue to recoup their investments.

Defense lawyers contend that the ruling was unnecessary because partners always are liable for a partnership's debts, including any judgments. "I don't think it really changes a thing," said Stuart L. Kadison of Los Angeles, a lawyer for Arthur Andersen. "They still have to win a case against Arthur Andersen for liability."

But the bondholders' attorney sought to make the partners defendants individually because the insurance coverage available to the three accounting firms would not cover all claims made in the cases.

The accounting firms are among a host of defendants sued in 17 class actions consolidated in Bilby's court. The suits contend that American Continental's former chairman, Charles H. Keating Jr., with the help of other defendants and politicians perpetrated a securities scheme that defrauded bondholders.

Among that group are more than 17,000 small investors who bought nearly $200 million in bonds through Lincoln's 29 Southern California branches. They have said that they were led to believe those bonds were safe or insured when, in fact, the bonds were risky and uninsured.

Keating, 66, was indicted in September on 24 counts of securities fraud and other violations related to the bond sales. He has pleaded not guilty.

Orange County Business

Making Taxes Work for You
CPA Helps Decode IRS Rules for Small-Business Owners

In the past decade there have been two major rewrites of the nation's income tax laws, the Economic Recovery Tax Act of 1981 and the Tax Reform Act of 1986.

In addition, Congress, the federal tax court and the Internal Revenue Service itself have amended, revised, updated, clarified, added to and/or subtracted from the tax codes hundreds of times.

Taxpayers and politicians argue whether the result really has been a reform of the nation's tax law, but just about everyone agrees that there certainly has not been any simplification.

As a result, there are dozens of little-known and often overlooked rules that can help taxpayers, especially owners of small businesses, minimize their tax bills, says Norman A. Barker, director of tax for the Orange County office of Ernst & Young in Newport Beach.

Barker, 42, earned a bachelor's degree in psychology at USC and then entered the university's law school,

NORMAN A. BARKER
Q&A

where he earned a law degree.

So, with that education, how did he become a certified public accountant specializing in tax issues?

Well, Barker's grandfather was a lawyer, but his father is a CPA. He decided to follow in both their footsteps.

A Southern California native, he had taken a few accounting courses at USC as an undergraduate and, in the summer of 1970, between his first and second years in law school, applied for a position in the tax department of the

Los Angeles office of Ernst & Whinney, the accounting firm. It became Ernst & Young last year in a merger with the Arthur Young & Co., another major accounting firm.

Barker worked full time while completing his law degree and then was shipped off to the University of Miami in Ohio for an intensive 10-week CPA course—his only accounting classes since his undergraduate years in the late 1960s.

"Then I came back, rented a cabin in the mountains and studied 25 hours a day for the CPA exam, which I took and passed on the first try in 1973," he said.

After stints at Ernst & Whinney offices in Los Angeles and Cleveland and at the firm's New York headquarters, Barker transferred to the Orange County office in 1980.

With the April 16 deadline for filing 1989 tax returns drawing near, Barker recently shared some of his thoughts on small-business tax matters with Times staff writer John O'Dell.

Q. The corporate tax guys at Beckman Instruments probably won't get much out of this, but they can afford to hire all the help they need. Share with us some 1989 tax-filing tips for small-business owners—the ones who should hire tax advisers but often can't afford to.

A. The most fundamental thing a small business can do is decide what form it will take. The rules taxing partnerships are radically different from the rules for corporations or sole proprietorships or any of the other forms a business can take. One of the most popular vehicles for small business is the S corporation. You have to elect to be an S corporation within the first 75 days of the beginning of your corporate year. It is a form that is very good for a lot of tax reasons. It also is a form that can be used to reduce FICA [Social Security] taxes for the self-employed.

Q. And as high as Social Security taxes are for the self-employed, that could be a big benefit. How does it work?

A. If you are working for your own S corporation, even if you are the owner and only employee, then you can limit the amount of salary you take out of the corporation and the self-employment [FICA] tax only applies to what you take out in salary.

Q. An example, please?

A. Let's say your business earns $200,000 for the year, although you can use any numbers you want. You could pay yourself a salary of $40,000, assuming that would be reasonable in relation to the services you perform for the business. Your self-employment tax would be on the $40,000 salary instead of on the $48,000 maximum taxable amount for FICA in 1989. That maximum jumps to $51,300 this year. The key here is that the salary has to be a reasonable amount for the services rendered. You couldn't pay yourself $10 and get away with it. In any event, with the S corporation as your employer, the total FICA tax can be less than paying the full self-employment rate of 13.02% for 1989 and 15.3% for 1990.

Q. What about other taxes?

A. Well, the federal corporate tax rate is 34%. That's much higher than the personal rate. But except in unusual circumstances, there is no federal corporate tax on an S corporation. The state tax is 2.5%, but that is pretty low. Also, the S corporation avoids some penalties that other types of corporations can face. There is no penalty for accumulated earnings or for excessive compensation, for instance.

(Continued on page 24)

(Continued from page 23)

Q. I have a feeling a lot of people who own their own businesses would argue vehemently that there is no such thing as excessive compensation.

A. One way a corporation's shareholder-employees used to drain the corporation of all of its income so it didn't have to pay any tax was to pay out all the corporate income as salaries to themselves. Sometimes, the amount of salary was more than the value of the services they provided. That still happens sometimes. But if the IRS determines that the salary paid is greater than the value of the service provided, it disallows the deduction for the excess amount. But that provision does not apply to an S corporation. So the owner or owners can draw down the entire income as salary.

Q. What, if anything, does the federal tax system do to encourage small-business formation?

A. Sadly, if you follow the letter and spirit of the law, most of the expenses incurred in starting your business cannot be deducted right away. They must be capitalized. If you hire an attorney to file your incorporation papers and do other pre-formation legal work, for instance, you cannot deduct on your first-year tax return what you paid the attorney. You must capitalize the amount and deduct it over a 60-month period. So you ultimately get the deduction, but it is stretched over five years. If the law were more friendly, you would get the deduction up front, when it would probably help the most.

Q. What is the rationale?

A. The theory is that the money you paid to get organized is not a cost that relates just to the income you earn in the first year but to income you'll earn in perpetuity. So the government makes you stretch out the deduction over 60 months. The same thing is true with start-up expenses. You hire employees, paint the shelves . . . and do things like that before you open your doors, and those costs have to be capitalized and amortized over five years.

Q. There are some tax benefits for hiring the hard-core unemployed, aren't there?

A. It is called the targeted jobs credit and it's a tax credit for businesses that hire people in one or more of nine different target groups, typically persons who are economically disadvantaged. They include economically disadvantaged Vietnam-era veterans and economically disadvantaged young people. Once you, as a business owner, get a certification from the state Employment Development Department that a person you have hired qualifies in one of these categories, you get a federal tax credit, computed at 40% of up to $6,000 of the person's first-year wages.

Q. Does this have to be a full-time employee?

A. No. And the tax credit can be pretty significant. It runs as high as $2,400 for an employee who makes $6,000 or more. And it adds up when you think of all the hotels, fast food places and other businesses that hire people who fit these targeted jobs categories. The credit was scheduled to expire on Dec. 31, but Congress extended it until Sept. 30, the end of the federal fiscal year.

Q. Why only nine months?

A. It is one of several things that were extended through September, which is the end of the government's budget year and the time when Congress typically acts on new tax laws. I believe it may be extended again in whatever tax measures Congress passes in September.

Q. How does the law treat business equipment—cash registers, machinery and the like?

A. Equipment is depreciated from the time it is placed in service. Before the Economic Recovery Tax Act of 1981, in Reagan's first year as President, you could write off most equipment over five

❝ Before 1981, you could write off most equipment over five years, but now the depreciation rules have some 130 different classifications. . . The tax code is a full employment act for bean counters. ❞

years. But now the depreciation rules have some 130 different classifications. Before I can tell you how long you must depreciate a certain piece of equipment, I have to look up what classification it belongs in. The tax code is a full employment act for bean counters.

Q. What about simpler things, like use of your personal car for business when the employer doesn't provide one, or when you are using your own car in a sole proprietorship.

A. You can get a benefit, but the record-keeping is a quagmire. There are two ways to deduct car expenses. You can take the standard mileage deduction for business use, which changes every year. Or you can keep track of actual expenses—gas, oil, repairs, maintenance, car washes and insurance—and you can depreciate the car's value and then compare those costs to the standard business use deduction and take whichever one is higher. And you can switch back and forth, using the standard deduction one year and the itemized the next. But you have to keep accurate records of your business mileage.

Q. How about home offices? Hasn't the IRS recently lightened up a bit on home office restrictions?

A. Home offices have to be used regularly and exclusively for business—

period. And you have to have a reason to have one. You can't just decide to set one up because you like to bring work home at night. There has been one change in the law, however. You used to have to meet clients in your home office and conduct the bulk of your business there for it to be deductible. Now the tax court has held that the home office only has to be the focal point of your business. A salesman who meets his customers at their place of business and who doesn't have a permanent office at company headquarters—for example, a regional representative for a company located in the East—can legitimately have a home office if that's where all the record-keeping, billing and dealing with the main office takes place.

Q. What's the tax treatment for business use of personal computers and other office equipment?

A. That's what is termed 'listed property,' and it is treated differently from business equipment. A computer, for example, can be used for personal and business reasons. So you start with the regular depreciation rules and then, for listed property, the deduction has been cut down. You can deduct the business cost but over a longer period of time, often as much as 12 years. And you have to keep very detailed records to prove what part of the use was business and what was personal. Remember, unless the IRS is charging fraud, the burden of proof in any dispute with the IRS is on you. And with things like cars and computers, the best way to prove business use is to keep an accurate log.

Q. What are some other things for the small-business person to know about?

A. Well, federal law gives a real benefit to the business owner who suffers a net operating loss for the year. You basically get a 19-year period to use the loss to offset profits. You can use it for the current year, carry it back three years and, if there is still any loss to account for, then you can carry it forward for up to 15 years. It was designed to help businesses with really cyclical income.

(Continued on page 25)

(Continued from page 24)

Q. How does the state treat operating losses?

A. California didn't allow any carry-back or carry-forward of losses until 1987. You didn't have to pay taxes in the year you took the loss, but that was it. In 1987, the state introduced a limited loss carry-forward for certain kinds of losses. But you still can't go back to prior years and use this year's loss to offset previously paid taxes. The way the law is worded, businesses with operating losses can carry 50% of those losses forward to offset profits for up to 15 years, or until they are absorbed.

Q. In your experience, what kinds of things on tax returns—short of outright fraud—typically raise red flags at the IRS?

A. For individuals, the first is a return on which income doesn't match the income reported to the IRS on 1099 forms. The 1099 is the statement of interest earnings, investment income, proceeds from real estate sales and other income that you get from banks, brokerages, escrow companies and clients for whom you've done work. They have to send a copy of that statement to the IRS, and if you report $100 in interest income on an account at your bank and the bank's 1099 says you earned $120, you will almost automatically get a letter about it from the IRS and the state because of their computerized programs for matching 1099s with individual returns.

Q. That kind of thing doesn't result in an audit, does it? Don't you just get a letter asking you to either explain the discrepancy or, if you agree with the IRS, to send a check for the back tax and late penalties?

A. Yes. But if you do it enough, or if a single mismatch is big enough—like you report $10 in interest and the bank says it was $10,000—that could get you audited. The IRS is also going to take notice of tax returns that are not self-explanatory. By that, I mean returns that lack the statements and schedules that support the numbers. Agents also will red-flag a return that shows a substantial business loss, one that wipes out the tax liability, or a file that has several years of consecutive business losses.

Q. They also watch charitable contribution claims pretty closely, don't they?

A. If you report contributions that are significant. There is a new form that you must file if you make a non-cash donation worth $500 or more. You have to itemize the property and give it a value. And if your donated property is worth $5,000 or more you have to have it

---

❛ There is a new form that you must file if you make a non-cash donation worth $500 or more. You have to itemize the property and give it a value. ❜

---

appraised by a professional appraiser. What gets some people is that if the recipient of a donated property sells it within two years, the charity must notify the IRS of the sales price. So if you donated a sailboat to UCI and valued it at $6,000 on your tax return and then UCI turns around and sells it for a quick $1,000, the IRS is going to want an explanation of the discrepancy. To keep your deduction, you're going to have to show that UCI sold it at an artificially low price and that your $6,000 value was the real value. Of course, sophisticated organizations that get a lot of donated property typically will not sell it until after two years has passed so they avoid reporting the sale to the IRS.

Q. With cash donations, if you don't have a receipt from the organization, is your canceled check enough proof for the IRS?

A. It is not a receipt, but it is typically accepted by the IRS as proof of payment.

Q. Are there benchmarks that the IRS uses in deciding whether your deductions, exemption claims, business losses or whatever are out of the ordinary?

A. The answer is absolutely yes. But what they are is a closely guarded secret. And they change every year. There are a lot of parameters in the IRS computer, and your name *will* get on a list if you go beyond them. But whether or not that triggers an audit depends on how high on the list your name goes.

Q. Finally, how long do you need to keep personal or business tax records?

A. The federal income tax statute of limitations is three years, but I recommend you keep them forever. The statute in California is four years and, in our business, we typically keep state and federal records for seven years because there is a provision in federal law that says if you forgot to include an item that is 25% or more of your gross income, then the statute is extended to six years. And, of course, there is no statute of limitations at all in cases of fraud or if you simply didn't file. They can go back as far as they like.

BRIEFCASE

TECHNOLOGY

Late Payments Cause Cash Flow Problem for Helionetics

Helionetics Inc., the Irvine manufacturer of computer workstation products, says it has approved a new payment schedule for a Brazilian customer that owes a company subsidiary $2.7 million.

E. Maxwell Malone, Helionetics president and chief executive, said the customer's failure to pay the overdue loan has created a cash flow problem for Helionetics and its Definicon International subsidiary.

But Malone said the customer, Marketta International Corp., owned by Francisco Fusco in Sao Paulo, Brazil, has failed to comply with past loan schedules and that there is no assurance that the payments—now due in increments to be paid no later than Feb. 28—will be received.

"It's agonizingly slow in getting payments," Malone said.

Helionetics' stock, traded on the American Stock Exchange, closed Monday at $1.25 per share, off 50 cents, or 28.6%.

In November, 1989, Marketta placed a $7.6-million order with Helionetics for equipment to convert personal computers into more powerful workstations. Malone said Marketta has made payments of $5 million, but Helionetics has refused to ship the equipment until the order is paid in full.

Malone said Monday that Marketta will make an initial payment of $350,000 by Jan. 31 and pay off the remainder a month later. He said Helionetics has arranged a $5-million line of credit that will become available upon receipt of the Marketta payment.

The delay has led to unspecified layoffs at Helionetics. In November, the company disclosed that its Xcell Circuit Technology subsidiary was closed after it was suspended from doing business with the government.

On Nov. 15, Helionetics was sued by John S. Abram, former president and chief operating officer of Definicon, who alleged that he was fired after he spoke out about financial irregularities.

Malone also confirmed that the company no longer has corporate liability insurance protecting its officers and directors. As a result, he said directors Charles Jobbins and William Duke have resigned as directors.

Malone also said Helionetics' Delta Electronic Controls subsidiary expects to receive an additional $1 million in orders this quarter to supply power conversion systems to the Air Force for Operation Desert Storm.

The systems will be installed in commercial airliners that the U.S. Air Force is converting into flying hospitals. The power conversion systems are necessary to power the hospital equipment needed for in-flight surgery, Malone said.

Helionetics lost $961,000 on revenue of $15 million for the nine months ended Sept. 30, contrasted with net income of $6.4 million on revenue of $15.4 million for the same period a year earlier.

Optimistic Fluor Raises Quarterly Dividend by 25%

■ **Economy:** The Irvine giant, citing a 35% jump in earnings, strong cash flow and 'favorable outlook,' will give stockholders a bigger return per share.

By DEAN TAKAHASHI
TIMES STAFF WRITER

IRVINE—In a statement of confidence about its business prospects, Fluor Corp. said Tuesday that it will increase its quarterly dividend to stockholders to 8 cents per share, a 25% increase.

The announcement came one day after the Irvine-based engineering and construction company reported a 35% jump in earnings for its year ended Oct. 31. The company said it was raising its dividend because of its higher earnings, strong cash flow and a "favorable outlook" for its business.

The increase in Fluor's dividend is unusual at a time when many U.S. companies are growing cautious about a slowing economy. Fluor has acknowledged that its domestic sales are sluggish but said its overseas business is growing.

Kathryn A. Maag, an analyst at the Chicago investment firm Duff & Phelps Inc., said she was not surprised by Fluor's announcement. She noted that an 8-cent-a-share cash dividend payment would total only $6 million a quarter, an insubstantial amount for a company with annual revenue of more than $7 billion.

"I think they're trying to communicate their confidence that they can sustain a given level of cash flow," Maag said. "Even if there is a severe recession, the dividend level is low enough where it should not be a problem for the company."

For its fiscal year ended Oct. 31, Fluor reported earnings of $146.9 million, up from $108.5 million. Revenue rose 18.6% to $7.45 billion from $6.28 billion in 1989.

The company has been benefiting from a revival of the international petrochemical production and processing business that was once its mainstay.

"We have in excess of $400 million in cash," said Deborah Land, a company spokeswoman.

"We base our dividend on Fluor's performance, and Fluor's performance has been very strong. So it made sense to raise [the dividend]."

Fluor stock closed Tuesday at $37.75, off $1.125 per share in New York Stock Exchange trading.

The dividends are payable on Jan. 16, 1991, to shareholders of record at the close of business on Dec. 26, 1990.

DEALS / ALLAN SLOAN
AT&T's Puzzling Accounting

What in the world is AT&T up to? The company seems to announce huge one-time losses every few years, almost like clockwork. You wonder when the next shoe will drop, and how big it will be. If this keeps on, AT&T is going to have to adopt the centipede as a corporate symbol.

Last month, the company announced that it was taking $4 billion worth of losses, which will wipe out most of its profit for the year. This makes three times in the eight years since the breakup of the Bell System that AT&T has announced three special losses, which now total around $14 billion. That's right, $14,000,000,000. A lot of zeros, isn't it?

Wall Street, in its wisdom, thought the $4-billion hit was just dandy, and ran AT&T stock up. Why? Because the Street felt that the writeoffs would increase AT&T's future earnings. Which they will. But this makes you wonder whether Wall Street's obsession with reported profits blinds it to underlying economic reality.

Because, you see, when you count the $4-billion hit—call it $2.64 billion after taxes—AT&T's earnings since the Bell breakup are much less than the dividends it has paid out. If you subtract the charge, $2.40 a share, AT&T's earnings since 1984 total $7.01 a share and its dividends $9.18.

In other words, AT&T has sliced $2 billion from its net worth—now about $13 billion—to pay its dividend. It even boosted its dividend last year. It's the corporate equivalent of eating into your seed corn.

Now that AT&T, the quintessential widows-and-orphans company, has committed itself to the cutthroat, high-risk computer business by buying NCR Corp., you wonder how long it can keep paying out more than it makes.

Enter Bernie Ragland, AT&T's chief accountant. Ragland, a bright and gracious fellow, spent two hours with me discussing the meaning of profit, how you decide what's a one-time loss and what's an operating expense, and other accounting metaphysics.

To grossly oversimplify, Ragland says the $6-billion 1986 loss, the $6.7-billion 1988 loss and this year's $4-billion loss were one-time-only events. Even though there has been a recurring pattern of non-recurring charges, Ragland argues that each charge was proper. Changing a 100-year-old company from a regulated monopoly into a competitor during an unsettled economic period like this one has required "more than the usual level of adjustment," Ragland argues.

The 1986 and 1988 writeoffs were caused by accounting changes, charges for trying to fix money-losing businesses and deciding that large parts of its long-distance network were obsolete.

This year, the company is charging $1.5 billion for expenses connected with buying NCR Corp., another $1.5 billion for trying once again to fix its money-losing business equipment business, $300 million for subsidy payments to a phone company in Alaska and $700 million for miscellaneous, most of which seems to be the cost of making lease payments on facilities that are empty or under-utilized.

Let's be sports and say that all $1.5 billion is money—for severance pay, employee moving costs and so on—that AT&T wouldn't have spent had it not bought NCR. Clearly, a non-recurring, one-time charge.

But some of the other $2.5 billion makes me wonder. Is AT&T taking charges that make this year's earnings look worse than they are and will make future earnings better?

It depends on how you look at things. Ragland concedes that if AT&T were stuck with a few surplus leased properties, it would charge the lease payments on them to operations, rather than taking one big charge. But because AT&T has lots of surplus leased space, it's taking a big charge now, which means smaller expenses
(Continued on page 37)

ALLAN SLOAN *is a financial columnist for Newsday in New York.*

Western Digital Sale of Network Unit Gets Final OK

■ **Computers:** The $33-million deal is thought to be crucial to company efforts to increase cash flow and meet loan agreements.

By DEAN TAKAHASHI
TIMES STAFF WRITER

IRVINE—Western Digital Corp., in an effort to raise some badly needed cash, said it has reached a final agreement to sell its computer network business to New York-based Standard Microsystems Corp. for $33 million.

In another development, Western Digital said British computer maker Amstrad plc has filed a $141-million lawsuit against the Irvine firm for allegedly supplying faulty computer disk drives in 1988 and 1989.

Western Digital officials said Amstrad's charges are unfounded and that the company is considering filing a countersuit. The Amstrad suit was filed Monday in federal court in Santa Ana.

The sale of the network business, which was announced as a tentative agreement in March, is expected to be completed on Sept. 27. The unit had annual sales of $115 million.

Analysts said the sale is crucial to Western Digital's efforts to improve its cash flow and to ensure that it can meet the terms of restructured loan agreements with its banks.

"Getting the $33 million in cash will be good news for them because they need the money," said Lawrence Borgman, an analyst at Dillon Read & Co. in New York. "This is a difficult quarter for them because of heavy [price cutting]."

Western Digital lost $26.5 million on revenue of $253.3 million for its fiscal fourth quarter ended June 30. In August, the company renegotiated its long-term debt with its lenders.

Western Digital, which makes personal computer components, said the network unit was not essential to its business strategy.

The company wants to become a supplier of products based on semiconductor technology, the tiny chips that serve as the engines of PCs. But it no longer wants to mount those chips on circuit boards, which is becoming an increasingly competitive business. The networking unit was mostly based on circuit board technology.

In addition to the cash payment, Western Digital will retain its accounts receivable for the networking unit, its existing product inventory and accounts payable at the sale's closing. Standard Microsystems, based in Hauppage, N.Y., will continue to work with Western Digital, including developing a new networking chip for the Irvine company. Analysts estimate those terms are worth $20 million to $30 million for Western Digital.

The Amstrad lawsuit claims that a now-obsolete line of Western Digital disk drives failed to meet the quality of Amstrad's previous supplier, Tandon Corp., which Western Digital acquired in March, 1989.

Amstrad filed a similar lawsuit Monday against Seagate Technology Inc., a hard disk drive manufacturer based in Scotts Valley, Calif.

Western Digital said Amstrad waited 18 months after delivery of the disk drives to notify it that the products did not meet quality requirements.

Western Digital stock fell 12.5 cents to $2.875 per share, a 52-week low, in New York Stock Exchange trading Tuesday.

General Electric Co. Plans to Take $1.8-Billion Charge

■ **Earnings:** The company says it is adopting a new method of accounting for retiree benefits.

From Associated Press

FAIRFIELD, Conn.—General Electric Co. announced Monday that it would restate its first-quarter earnings to reflect a one-time, $1.8-billion charge for adopting a new accounting standard for retiree benefits.

The change is expected to result in a first-quarter per share loss of 85 to 95 cents, according to GE spokesman George Jamison.

The after-tax charge on earnings represents less than 10% of GE's equity and will not affect cash flow, the company said. Moody's Investors Service and Standard & Poors have both informed GE that the adjustment will have no impact on its top-level debt ratings.

GE will adopt in the third quarter Financial Accounting Standard No. 106, which requires a new method of accounting for retiree benefits other than pensions. The rule, which must be implemented by all U.S. companies before the end of 1993, requires the companies to restate their first-quarter results, Jamison said. General Electric is one of the first companies to implement the new standard.

GE earnings for the first quarter totaled $999 million, or $1.15 per share, on revenue of $13.3 billion. That compared to earnings of $950 million, or $1.06 per share, on revenue of $12.6 billion for the same period in 1990.

GE said earnings-per-share calculated before the one-time charge are expected to increase in the third quarter and fourth quarter and for the full 1991 fiscal year. The second quarter will be unaffected, Jamison said.

Sir Speedy Pays $4 Million for Accounting Franchiser

By CRISTINA LEE
TIMES STAFF WRITER

LAGUNA HILLS—Sir Speedy Inc., a quick-printing franchiser based here, said Monday it has acquired Comprehensive Accounting Corp., an Illinois franchiser of accounting services, for more than $4 million in cash.

The sale, which includes certain franchise contracts, trademarks, trade secrets and accounts receivable, will mark Sir Speedy's entry into the financial services industry.

Comprehensive operates 223 franchise outlets throughout the United States. The outlets are staffed by certified accountants who provide monthly accounting, bookkeeping, tax and business consulting services primarily to small and medium-size businesses. Founded in 1949, the company had revenue of $10 million in 1989.

Comprehensive plans to move its headquarters from Aurora, Ill., to Carlsbad in San Diego County in November, said Don Lowe, Sir Speedy president and chief executive. He said about half of Comprehensive's 37 employees have agreed to be relocated to California and 20 more employees will be hired by the year's end.

The company eventually will change its name to Comprehensive Business Services Inc. Sir Speedy plans to merge the operations of its subsidiary, California Franchise Industries Inc., into the new company, Lowe said.

"What we liked about [Comprehensive] is that their customers and ours are about the same—small and mid-size companies—and we're both in the franchising business," Lowe said.

C. Robert Wissler, a Sir Speedy senior vice president, has been named president and chief operating officer of Comprehensive, which will be operated as a subsidiary of Sir Speedy.

Accounting Changes Aid Hammond

■ **Finance:** Company reports a profit of $412,000 for fiscal 1990; it lost nearly $1.1 million the year before.

By JOHN O'DELL
TIMES STAFF WRITER

NEWPORT BEACH—Taking advantage of two significant accounting changes that enabled it to boost its income, the Hammond Co. reported a $412,000 profit for its fiscal 1990, contrasted with a net loss of nearly $1.1 million for the previous year.

But the publicly owned mortgage banking firm's financial statement shows that without the $535,000 it gained in the third quarter from the accounting changes, it would have lost $122,517 for the year ended March 31.

Hammond officials say, however, that the company fared well in a year in which real estate sales throughout the United States fell substantially from the record levels established in prior years. The company's sales for 1990 were down 3% to $19.8 million, from $20.4 million a year earlier.

The fiscal 1990 operating loss was only half the operating loss of the previous year, said John Bastis, Hammond's executive vice president and chief financial officer.

Bastis said the company's 1989 loss was the result of several unusual factors including a one-time, $450,000 loss from the company's failed attempt to acquire a savings and loan and a $400,000 loss from unpaid mortgage insurance claims.

Without those items, Bastis said, Hammond's 1989 result would have been a $225,000 loss, or slightly more than twice the fiscal 1990 operating loss.

For fiscal 1990, Hammond adopted new accounting procedures that allowed it to reduce its reserves for federal income taxes and to book the net savings as a one-time gain of $281,000 and to realize a one-time gain of $254,000 by changing the way it depreciates the value of income from loan servicing contracts.

Bastis said Hammond has been able to pare its losses in the midst of a sales downturn by trimming operating expenses.

For fiscal 1990, he said, Hammond realized considerable savings by closing seven money-losing offices. The company operates 16 offices, including a new one recently opened in Sacramento.

For the fourth quarter, the company lost $451,490, contrasted with a year-earlier loss of $855,684. Sales dipped slightly to $4 million from $4.1 million a year earlier.

Air Force Lied About B-1 Costs, GAO Study Says

■ **Aerospace:** The controversial report blasts AF accounting practices as shoddy. It also charges that there were billions in cost overruns on the F-15 and F-16 jet fighters.

By RALPH VARTABEDIAN
TIMES STAFF WRITER

The Air Force understated its cost on the B-1 bomber by $7.5 billion and on two other aircraft programs by an additional $18 billion, according to a draft General Accounting Office report that found that the Air Force's accounting practices have "significant internal control weaknesses."

The GAO disclosed, for example, that when the Air Force Space Division in Los Angeles found a $2.4-billion discrepancy in its accounting books, it simply made an "unsupported and arbitrary" adjustment to get the books to balance.

The controversial report, which was the culmination of a three-year investigation, elicited a sharply worded statement by the Air Force, which "had serious disagreements with the content of the draft report and the handling of the audit. GAO's findings are fundamentally misdirected."

But some members of Congress reacted with outrage to the findings and vowed to hold hearings to develop new laws to strengthen the government's financial management. Rep. John Dingell (D-Mich.), whose staff obtained and leaked an executive summary of the unpublished draft report, said the findings "would be unbelieveable had we not seen firsthand the chaos in Air Force management."

A number of the GAO disclosures are sure to prompt serious concerns through-

out Congress, including the disclosure about the cost for 100 B-1 bombers. The report states that the cost of the bomber was represented as $23 billion, but the actual cost was $7.5 billion more. If that is confirmed, it would mean the B-1 exceeded the cost cap that the Pentagon guaranteed to Congress.

In addition, the report said the F-15 jet fighter cost was understated by $8.3 billion and the F-16 was understated by $9.9 billion. The gaps are even wider when research and development is included, it said.

One specific problem is the service's failure to track military-owned hardware that is held by defense contractors. For example, $630 million worth of satellites paid for by the Air Force but in the possession of defense contractors were "not recorded in any Air Force property or accounting system," the report said.

The report by the GAO, which is an investigatory arm of Congress, was titled "Financial Management—Billion Dollar Decisions Made Using Inaccurate and Unreliable Air Force Data."

An Air Force spokeswoman said the service received the report Feb. 1 and has not had time to respond to specific allegations. In a lengthy rebuttal, however, the service claimed the GAO attempted to apply accounting principles used by profit-making corporations. It said the GAO concept for accounting "has not been accepted by the Congress or the executive branch."

The statement added that the report fails to recognize the Air Force's "fund control system" used to report on the status of its funds to Congress. And the statement concludes, "The GAO report creates a faulty impression of waste and mismanagement. That perception is simply not true." The Defense Department may be less inclined to object to the GAO findings or to future reforms, according to a knowledgeable source.

Longtime internal Air Force critic A. Ernest Fitzgerald, remarked, "Missing a few billion dollars? What the hell."

Fitzgerald, the management systems deputy in the Office of the Assistant Secretary of the Air Force for financial management, has railed for years that the defense procurement system has a "weakness in our protections against collusive fraud." He charged that what few internal checks and balances existed in the Pentagon's financial system were watered down by the Packard Commission reforms, implemented in an executive directive in 1986.

Julian Epstein, the staff director for the House Government Operations Committee, said, "If the report is true, it indicates very serious problems in the Air Force in terms of wasting billions of taxpayers dollars." The committee, along with Dingell's powerful Committee on Energy and Commerce and the House Armed Services Committee, may hold hearings.

In a letter, Dingell said the $2.4-billion accounting error committed by the Air Force Space Division is "five times the entire

(Continued on page 35)

Effects Look Better on Screen Than Balance Sheet

Simi Valley: Although Dream Quest Images won an Oscar for its optical wizardry in 'The Abyss,' the company actually lost money on the project.

By JOHN MEDEARIS
TIMES STAFF WRITER

"I really truthfully wish there was no business aspect to it," said Hoyt Yeatman, talking about Dream Quest Images, the Simi Valley motion picture special effects company he owns with two partners.

The boyish, 35-year-old special effects artist, wearing jeans and a loose-collared shirt, bubbles over with excitement when he talks about creating the illusion that models hanging on wires are really submarines in the deep, but not so much when the topic is balance sheets.

"That's not my area," he said.

Visual effects work is a business, however—and a tough one, where even artistic triumphs can entail financial losses. Take, for example, Dream Quest's work on "The Abyss."

Yeatman shared an Oscar this year with three others for visual effects in the film—which included Dream Quest's creation of realistic underwater action scenes with computer-manipulated models.

But despite the boost it gave Dream Quest's reputation, "The Abyss" must have caused Dream Quest's accountants to fret. The project actually cost 5% to 8% more to complete than Dream Quest was paid, according to Keith Shartle, executive producer of feature film projects at the company.

The Simi Valley company—owned by Yeatman and partners Tom Hollister and Fred Iguchi—had already done the visual effects for movies from "Nightmare on Elm Street 4" and "Gremlins" to "Big Business" and "Fat Man and Little Boy."

Winning the Oscar was a breakthrough for the company that helped put Dream Quest in the visual effects big league with companies such as George Lucas' Industrial Light and Magic (ILM). "I consider our main competition to be Dream Quest," said Scott Ross, ILM's vice president and general manager.

That means Dream Quest is one of only a handful of companies that can hope to bid for work on giant special effects movies.

In fact, only two companies—ILM and Dream Quest—were considered to do the effects for "Total Recall," said Buzz Feitshans, producer of the upcoming Arnold Schwarzenegger release, which is set on Mars. The film's $50-million budget included a whopping $8 million for visual effects, according to Feitshans. Dream Quest's Eric Brevig supervised the shooting and post-production optical work on all but 11 of the 120 different special effects shots for the movie. ILM did the opticals on the rest.

Recognition has swelled Dream Quest's revenues by 50% a year for the last five years, according to Shartle. In 1989, Dream Quest's sales—which come about 60% from feature films and 40% from television commercials—were in the range of $10 million to $20 million, Shartle said. The company as a whole is profitable, despite the loss on "The Abyss," Yeatman said.

But the more challenging and complicated Dream Quest's assignments become, the more difficult it can be to make a profit on them. The basic problem is that visual effects aren't widgets—they can't be stamped out the same way every time.

Take, for example, the script for "The Abyss," which called for some underwater prospectors to encounter shimmering aliens deep in the ocean.

The aliens were built out of clear urethane with optical fibers woven through to make them luminescent. The puppets were also mechanized to make their wings beat "Peter Pan-like," as Yeatman put it. After being filmed, the image of the aliens was to be essentially superimposed onto to footage of the human characters in the movie.

But Yeatman said the mechanical wings just didn't look right flapping loosely in the air. On the other hand, director James Cameron discovered that the aliens' wings beat angelically when the puppets were held underwater, bobbing "like a toilet plunger, up and down."

Because special effects cameras shouldn't be submerged in water, filming the aliens that way entailed building a clear plexiglass tank—the alien went inside and the camera stayed outside. And to create the impression that the alien was hovering in place—even though it was actually being plunged up and down to make its wings beat—the camera and alien had to be attached so they bobbed together.

Even then, the work wasn't done. The plexiglass tank, it turned out, created an optical distortion that had to be corrected with a specially built lens.

"I would say that added several weeks of shooting," Yeatman said. And every week of extra

(Continued on page 35)

Balance Sheet—*continued from page 34*

shooting increased Dream Quest's losses. Even so, Yeatman said, the result was worth it.

Although their work is valued, special effects companies can't just hand a tab to the producer and expect full payment. Many visual effects contracts pay only a fixed fee, and although the fee can be renegotiated if directors and producers make more demands, the fixed amount doesn't always cover costs. Some contracts cover costs plus a percentage fee, but the profit in such deals obviously depends on what gets counted as a cost.

The fees are large. But Yeatman said the money "comes in in wheelbarrows but it goes right back out."

Mostly it goes back into the hands of dozens of special effects workers—matte painters, film editors and others. Shartle estimated that at least 70% of fees for special effects go to labor. Make that about 80%, ILM's Ross said.

"We're talking over 100, 120 people working for a year," Yeatman said, adding that the special effects crew can be bigger than the live action crew. "People are working a minimum of 10 to 14 hours per day—many times, six-day weeks—and often, towards the end, seven-day weeks."

All that labor is necessary because of the nature of special effects work.

"You're constantly being asked to do something you haven't done before," Shartle said. Then thinking some more, he added: "You're usually being asked to do something *no one's* done before."

An example is the matter of filming action scenes involving several submarines and underwater crafts at once for "The Abyss." Clearly, it wasn't possible to build full-scale versions and film them at sea. The only option was to use models.

But director Cameron insisted that because the action was set thousands of feet under water—where no sunlight penetrates—the only light visible could be cast from one craft onto another.

Unfortunately, that ruled out the standard method of creating the illusion that ships are flying or floating past each other, which involves shooting models separately and adding their images, one by one, to the background. That wouldn't work for "The Abyss" because Cameron's lighting called for the models actually to be next to each other when filmed.

To control many models at once, Dream Quest built a gantry system—a sort of mechanized puppet-master—from which to hang them. To record the models' motions so they could be repeated or just slightly changed, they devised special computer hardware that could keep track of more motions than previous hardware. The gantry alone, which Dream Quest may not have use for again, cost $120,00.

Yet even the gantry and the computer didn't do the whole trick. That's because the wires from which the models dangled were too thin to carry electricity to light the ships. And batteries placed in each model kept running down during extended filming.

So Yeatman and his crew installed radio receivers in the models, which allowed them to turn the lights off every time the camera shutter closed—effectively doubling the life of the batteries.

"It was an overwhelming film in general," Yeatman said.

It was a long way to the Oscar from Yeatman's start in visual effects, working on "Close Encounters of the Third Kind."

While still at UCLA film school, Yeatman's job on that Steven Spielberg film was small. "They needed somebody to baby-sit the camera," Yeatman said. "I didn't know what I was doing. I just sat there and made sure it didn't burn down."

But after working on "Star Trek—The Motion Picture," Yeatman and five friends decided to start their own tiny special effects company in West Los Angeles. After investing $1,500 each, they converted the garage of a house into a studio and set up shop, leaping at any opportunity they could get, such as creating futuristic computer-screen characters for "Blade Runner" and making clay balls seem to whirl around like planets for "E.T."

Shartle and Yeatman say they hope Dream Quest has come far enough since those days that it can afford to pick its challenges. "Now it's not quite so hard-nosed a business," Shartle said. "We might pass up a project because it's something that we've already done."

Air Force—*continued from page 33*

drug abuse education budget of the U.S. government." Dingell called for a 10% to 15% cut in the Pentagon acquisition budget.

The GAO found that when the Air Force recently submitted financial reports to the Treasury it neglected to include $25 billion in assets and counted $10 billion in other assets twice.

The service lacks accurate data for "almost all of its non-cash assets, such as inventory, equipment, aircraft and missiies," despite the fact that its bases represent 16% of the real property of the entire U.S. government, the GAO said.

It noted that the Air Logistics Centers, which hold inventories of spare parts, have record-keeping deficiencies that "contribute to $18 billion of inventory in excess of requirements."

S&P Hits Planned Rule Change on Medical Benefits Accounting

From Associated Press

NEW YORK—Standard & Poor's Corp., a major credit-rating agency, said Tuesday that a proposed accounting rule for retirees' medical benefits would be prone to large errors and would distort companies' balance sheets.

The proposed rule would make companies face up to reality by listing the future cost of retirees' medical benefits as a liability on their books.

Rough estimates of the new liabilities range from $400 billion to $2 trillion for all U.S. companies.

"It's not the concept that's the problem so much as the implementation," Solomon Samson, a Standard & Poor's managing director, said in an interview. "You may be doing yourself more of a disservice, even though the objective is very noble."

Samson said Standard & Poor's would stick to its own method of estimating how retirees' medical expenses would affect credit-worthiness.

Companies that promised generous medical benefits to employees upon retirement are seeking changes in the accounting proposal, which would force firms to slash their reported profits by billions of dollars.

Standard & Poor's criticism, which first surfaced in a Wall Street Journal story Tuesday, was the severest yet in the ongoing debate.

Officials at Ford Motor Co. and American Telephone & Telegraph Co. said Tuesday in phone interviews that they support the change in principle but believe that it is too stringent as proposed.

Listing future medical benefits as a liability will sting all companies but especially ones that gave their employees better retirement medical benefits because it seemed cheaper in the short run than paying higher wages and salaries.

Hardest hit will be smokestack industries such as auto makers and steelmakers that have generous benefits packages and growing ranks of retirees, combined with slow growth or no growth in revenue.

Lincoln Case—*continued from page 2*

by the Department of Justice" in a criminal action, not a civil case, Lerach said. He said $26 million in settlements with two law firms has already been negotiated in class-action suits filed in Orange County.

Van de Kamp said he considered the suit complementary rather than a duplication.

"I am here today to announce we're trying to get the bondholders' money back," he said.

> 'If investors had known the truth, no one would have invested a dime in those bonds.'
>
> **JOHN K. VAN DE KAMP**
> *California attorney general*

Money Store—
continued from page 12

reported profits, those profits are real, and the money will in fact show up. And while the company has to buy back more loans than usual, it's still solidly profitable and is selling an increasing number of loans in ways that don't require it to buy them back.

Fine. But given the murkiness of Money Store's profit statement and the increase in bad loans, this is a stock for people willing to take big risks. It's not something you buy to get a piece of Phil Rizzuto.

Auditors—*continued from page 9*

good knowledge of the banking industry and banking law. That's being stressed quite heavily. Auditing firms also are making sure they follow generally accepted auditing standards. There are, for example, peer group reviews in which other auditing firms look at the way a particular accounting firm audits. And, as I mentioned earlier, there have been certain reporting standards that outline what auditors must do in order to perform a sound audit.

Q. Are there other issues the accounting profession faces beyond the litigation and the S&L crisis?

A. Yes, I would say that one of the biggest issues auditors are facing and will face in the future is the big explosion of computerized information. Putting information on computers opens the possibility for misstatements of information and irregularities or illegal acts. It's very difficult for one person or several people to try to understand or process the amount of information that computers can generate. So auditors are continually trying to upgrade their knowledge on how to audit this kind of information. One thing the auditors have done of late is to develop so-called expert systems that help guide them through audits. In fact, Coopers & Lybrand has a very well-known expert systems package that they use.

Q. How much faith can the public put in audited financial statements?

A. If you look at it from a strictly statistical point of view, you would have to conclude that most audited financial statements by Big 6 firms are reliable. Studies have shown that most audited statements are very reliable. Banks, which are the biggest users of specially audited financial statements, rely on them in making loans. Investment bankers rely on them in advising clients. Audited financial statements are used as a basis for a company's future performance. Also, in the savings and loan and banking industries, there are federal and state auditors who do a very detailed audit of these institutions. In the case of the Lincoln Savings & Loan problem, some of the problems must be shared with the government in that the federal auditors did in fact find some irregularities. However, due to downward pressure by certain political entities, these auditors were not able to put Lincoln onto a problem list.

Q. They were not able to push corrective measures?

A. Exactly. Now bear in mind that the federal auditors work in conjunction with the independent auditors. They share information, and this, of course, improves the auditing process. So in some cases, if you have top regulatory agencies making policy statements that say, 'Look, this is a sound institution,' the independent auditors are relying on the federal professionals who are very adept at auditing from an internal perspective or from the federal government's perspective. When you have breakdowns in that system, it could lead to a bad audit or it could short-circuit auditing procedures in gathering information about such things as loan portfolios. At Lincoln, outside auditors relied on certain documented information that they believed was legitimate.

AT&T—*continued from page 28*

(and higher profits) in the future.

Why do you write off lots of leases as a one-time loss when you wouldn't write off a few leases? Ragland's answer: There are so many of these facilities that their cost makes it difficult for investors to divine AT&T's true profitability. He gives the same answer for the decision to make a one-time charge for five years of special payments to the Alaska phone company, rather than charging the payments to operating income each year.

And because AT&T has been trying to fix its money-losing business equipment operation for years, I think you can argue that some or all of the $1.5 billion in charges are recurring costs that should be charged to operations, not one-time charges. Ragland disagrees.

Answers Ragland, rhetorically: "Is the best way to inform investors to dribble these charges out over three or four years, or to report the $4 billion in the third quarter and explain clearly what it is?" He thinks that the charge is the way to go—but then, again, he should. Ragland and AT&T are doing what I would do in their place—taking the most favorable accounting treatment they can get.

But by doing that, I think AT&T has blurred the distinction between operating losses and one-time losses. If I were a betting man, I'd say that big non-recurring losses are going to keep right on recurring. My favorite candidate for the next one is NCR, which has already announced that its earnings projections were too high. Not a good sign.

So don't be surprised if you hear another AT&T shoe drop in 1992 or 1993. Tell the graphic designers to start work on the centipede.

Thump! Thud, thump, thud! Thump . . .